Selling School

Selling School

The Marketing of Public Education

Catherine DiMartino
Sarah Butler Jessen

Foreword by Christopher Lubienski

TEACHERS COLLEGE PRESS

TEACHERS COLLEGE | COLUMBIA UNIVERSITY
NEW YORK AND LONDON

Published by Teachers College Press, 1234 Amsterdam Avenue, New York, NY 10027

Cover design by Holly Grundon Design. Cover photos by shauni and PetrStransky via iStock by Getty Images.

Library of Congress Cataloging-in-Publication Data is available at loc.gov

Names: Dimartino, Catherine, author. | Jessen, Sarah Butler, author.
Title: Selling school : the marketing of public education / Catherine DiMartino, Sarah Butler Jessen ; Foreword by Christopher Lubienski.
Description: New York : Teachers College Press, [2018] | Includes bibliographical references and index. |
Identifiers: LCCN 2018001357 (print) | LCCN 2018006456 (ebook) | ISBN 9780807776780 (ebook) | ISBN 9780807758885 (pbk.) | ISBN 9780807758892 (hardcover)
Subjects: LCSH: Education—Marketing—Methodology. | Public schools—Public relations. | Educational fund raising.
Classification: LCC LB2847 (ebook) | LCC LB2847 .D55 2018 (print) | DDC 371.01—dc23
LC record available at https://lccn.loc.gov/2018001357

ISBN 978-0-8077-5888-5 (paper)
ISBN 978-0-8077-5889-2 (hardcover)
ISBN 978-0-8077-7678-0 (ebook)

Printed on acid-free paper
Manufactured in the United States of America

25 24 23 22 21 20 19 18   8 7 6 5 4 3 2 1

Contents

Foreword

Is it true that "image is everything"? In a famous advertising campaign from the 1990s, tennis star Andre Agassi sold cameras for Canon with that double entendre; the fact that the camera company chose someone known perhaps more for his flair than for his athletic victories may have underlined its point. The phrase may have foreshadowed our current cultural condition, where image is indeed everything on social media and in politics. Now professional image managers run advertising campaigns not only for commercial enterprises like grocery stores and used-car lots, but for institutions and efforts previously seen as beyond the purview of markets, such as churches, hospitals, and—increasingly—education.

Agassi, like many other celebrities, would go on to establish charter schools, lending his name and brand to seeding these new types of public schools. While people take different positions on charters, few would argue with the fact that schools such as these have done much to bring choice and competition into K–12 education. While choice and competition can have their advantages, they also incentivize efforts toward school marketing that in turn may divert school funds away from instruction and toward advertising budgets. This is particularly ironic given the "65% Solution"—mandating that at least 65% of school funds be spent in the classroom—pushed a few years ago by some of the same education reformers who are also advocates for markets in education. However, some see this as a good sign, that organizations prioritize their missions and seek consumers. But this trend in education also raises important issues: Does school marketing help level the already unequal playing fields of education and the information about education options? Does it provide parents with useful and accurate information for making school choices? What does this mean for school effectiveness?

These questions were brought home for me the first time I walked into a large-chain charter school in Michigan. The school's slick brochure showed students who looked nothing like the children I was seeing in the halls, at least in terms of the racial profile of the school. Later, a local public district administrator explained to me how, in competing with charters and other districts for students, he was now advertising his schools on an adult-jazz format radio station and how such ads paid for themselves with the per-pupil funding new recruits would bring. At the same time, a private school administrator told me that it would look bad if his school took out advertisements (it was unbecoming for an institution of their standing to resort to crass commercialism), although they had an amazing multimedia packet for prospective parents and required students to wear school-crested uniforms when on fieldtrips to make a good public impression. Other activities, such as school plays and sporting events, were now seen as part of larger marketing strategies for some schools. Administrators, teachers, and students were cast as key elements of such strategies, whether they wanted to be or not. These sea changes in the thinking on education are evident wherever markets have reorganized the education sector in their own image, from Chile to New Zealand, and across levels from preschool through higher education.

As market mechanisms like choice and competition further penetrate the education sector, a strategic response such as education marketing takes on greater significance not just for schools and parents, but also for researchers. As schools are increasingly positioned to act as businesses, the change in how we view schools suggests not just a new vocabulary for discussing education, but a new set of underlying assumptions for how education should be organized. Concepts that were previously largely foreign in the sector are increasingly commonplace. As you will see in this book, issues like branding and image management are not only being used in education, but are also seen as crucial to the effective operation of educational organizations. Yet such changes come with a shift in the roles for people involved in education. Families are now customers, school leaders are now brand managers, teachers and students play their parts in marketing strategies.

Earlier generations of work in this area was largely of the how-to variety: how districts could engage in public relations and how schools could foster community engagement. The question that motivated my own interest in this area focused on how marketing strategies could help expose the incentive structures undergirding local education markets: What does school marketing tell us about how schools perceive and respond to their competitors, potential clients, and contexts?

I am pleased that smart scholars such as Catherine DiMartino and Sarah Butler Jessen have pushed forward this important line of inquiry. In this comprehensive and thoughtful analysis, they dig deep into the rise of advertising in education (or *advertising*, as they call it), thoroughly investigating incentives, actors, strategies, and content. They are right in their prescient discussion of the muddling of public and private models in public education through marketing. In some respects, this is exactly the point of market-oriented reforms. Policies promoting choice and competition are meant to blur the traditional boundaries between public and private sectors. Reformers argued that public education is incapable of reforming itself, and needed to be infused with market mechanisms in order to bring consumer-oriented discipline and accountability to the public sector. While my own work and the work of others challenge the assumptions in that logic, the rise of marketing shows that these mechanisms are taking hold and becoming embedded in the institutions and operations of our education system. But will it help schools improve? Will it help families find the best options for their children? Perhaps most important, will it increase equity by supplying families marginalized in the current system with better information for finding better options for their children? Or will it instead accelerate the segregation of public education by facilitating the sorting of families into groups that, to use marketing terms, share "affinities" and "preferences"?

Which brings us back to the question of "image." New technologies have led to an explosion of information in recent years, including much that is "fake." Large percentages of the population are taken in by marketing campaigns for questionable remedies, junk science, and deplorable politicians whose images are managed by their handlers. In some regard these are simply examples of markets at work—that is, people choosing from sets of options promoted by marketers. Some would argue that the market is also the answer to these abuses, that more and better information—often in the form of earning trust for one's brands as competing providers are subjected to the discipline of consumers who won't be fooled again—will eventually root out misrepresentation and expose bad providers. However, as long as we see the success of Fox News, InfoWars, and late-night infomercials, there are doubts about the ability of markets to police themselves, whether in ideas or education, and there is substantial concern about the equity effects of requiring busy families to determine the validity of different marketing claims. Increasingly, image is everything—including a potential obstacle to useful information.

Christopher Lubienski

Acknowledgments

Many people helped us write this book. First, we must thank Dr. Janelle Scott, who brought us together. Janelle chaired both of our dissertations and fostered our mutual interest in market-based education reforms. We are grateful for her continued support and guidance as we pursue our own research interests.

Our home institutions provided valuable administrative and technical support. We are thankful for our colleagues at the University of Southern Maine, Bowdoin, and St. John's University who offered insightful feedback and shared their own experiences with branding and marketing in education.

We also benefitted from the expertise of fellow educational researchers, colleagues from across the United States who acted as thought partners and critical friends as we worked through early drafts of this book. In particular, Dr. Christopher Lubienski at Indiana University, Dr. Gary Anderson at New York University, and Samuel Abrams at the National Center for the Study of Privatization in Education at Teachers College provided early encouragement for our research on market-based education reforms.

We are also both fortunate to have wonderful students who supported our research. Joe Sherlock from Bowdoin and Christian Toala from St. John's University provided essential research support to this project; we are grateful for their interest and dedication to the high-quality scholarship we present in this book.

We interviewed many people for this project. We are deeply indebted to all of our participants. We thank our participants from New Orleans: teachers who spoke to us during their few, precious hours of free time in the evenings and on weekends. We are also grateful for the time that the marketing executives made for us during business hours and their willingness to share their experiences with us.

We would be remiss to leave out Brian Ellerbeck, our editor at Teachers College Press, who brought the book idea to us! Brian's encouragement and critical feedback were instrumental to the formation of this book.

Last but not least, we are grateful for our partners who encouraged and supported the creation of this book in so many ways. We appreciate their belief in the book and their commitment, themselves, to building a more just and equitable education system.

   We wrote this book for fellow parents, teachers, administrators, researchers, policymakers, and our own children—we have five between us—to shed light on the changing educational landscape. In this book, we aspire to clearly and vividly present the implications of market-based education reform for all stakeholders, to make sense of these profound changes to public education. We hope that this book encourages policymakers, parents, and practitioners to pause and take note of the current state of "edvertising" and school choice, to carefully consider whether this is the education system we want for our children and our nation.

Selling School

From "KIPP-Notizing" to an Edvertising Industry

Ultimately, a brand is a promise that we make to everyone in the team and family: KIPPsters, families, teachers, staff, community member, board members, funders, and supporters. The promise tells people, "This is what you can expect from us." Maintaining a strong brand is all about keeping our promises, but another part of a strong brand is consistency. It's important that we're all talking and messaging about KIPP in the same way, so that people recognize us as one organization. . . . We also believe in having a strong and consistent KIPP national brand, because that helps up recruit the best talent and support we need to give our KIPPsters a great education. Our brand has a lot of touch points: our website, t-shirt, written materials, stickers, our Twitter account, and even the way we answer the phone are all part of KIPP's brand. . . . Upholding the KIPP brand is especially important as we continue to grow as a network. A new KIPP school begins only with the reputation of the KIPP national brand before it builds one of its own. So we need to take care of our brand and keep it strong.

—KIPP Branding Video, KIPP website

In October of 2002, Donald Fisher—founder of Gap, Inc. and burgeoning venture philanthropist—donated $8 million to the Knowledge is Power Program (KIPP) Foundation. His purpose: pushing KIPP Public Charter Schools to expand to the national stage (Hendrie, 2002). KIPP, which was gaining rapidly in popularity in the years preceding this announcement, managed several charter schools under the KIPP moniker, including the famous flagship schools in Texas and New York City. The co-founders, David Levin and Michael Feinberg, were making headlines by promoting their new model of education into the popular culture in places like *60 Minutes;* the successes at these schools were widely lauded. Leading an organizational shift in the charter movement, KIPP had recently created a formal management organization to centralize operations. Mr. Fisher's donation would allow the newly formed KIPP Foundation, a charter management organization (CMO), to open 20 new schools per year in locations across the country. In announcing his gift, Mr. Fisher commented: "I see [KIPP] as a national brand. . . . We want to run this like a business so we can replicate this throughout the United States" (Hendrie, 2002). According to Hendrie (2002), in response, Feinberg confirmed: "Our goal is to KIPP-notize the country."

These two brief statements would foreshadow a sea change in public education. In the years since, branding and marketing have become keys to building public and political buy-in to educational models, institutions, and, in many cases, educational policies themselves. Much of this buy-in has been promoted through the media (Lubienski & Weitzel, 2010); the message is as important as the mission.

In Mr. Fisher's statement, the emphasis was placed on reframing educational companies by developing their "national brand," particularly as a component of the perhaps more critical desire to replicate these models as a franchise, as is done in the private sector. Simultaneously, there was a rhetorical shifting of the goal of education ever so slightly from a focus on educational pedagogy or curricular innovations, or even organizational structure, to more superficial image management: "KIPP-notizing." With these modifications, "edvertising"—the combined practice of marketing, branding, and advertising in education—began to take center stage in public education.

Within a short time, the edvertising industry has erupted in public education. KIPP is not alone, of course, in shepherding this movement—although, as we will see, they play a prominent role as a brand leader in the industry. Other educational organizations have quickly and eagerly followed suit, creating an entire edvertising industry. Charter management organizations, like Success Academy Charter Schools, Achievement First Public Schools, the Noble Network, and Uncommon Schools, to name a few, have ratcheted up their branding and marketing efforts. Many of the more organized networks now have multi-person, in-house marketing teams to ensure their organization's brand success and to maintain social media campaigns. These teams consist of experts in communications, graphic design, copy writing, and advertising. Some of these organizations have branding manuals, which clearly lay out their expectations around brand fidelity, and accompanying management-run compliance teams to audit individual schools in their networks.

More recently, public school districts have responded to this increased emphasis on image management. St. Louis, Denver, Grand Rapids, New York City, Cincinnati, Columbus, and Austin all reported using public school district funds to advertise their schools (Basco, 2016; Samuels, 2012; Sparling, 2016). However, as we will see, many of these marketing roles are critically different from those at the educational management organizations, which are more proactive in promoting and shaping the message of institutions, rather than serving a reactive or even purely informational role.

It is not only school management organizations that have begun to focus on edvertising practices, however. Teacher and principal recruiting organizations, such as Teach for America and New Leaders, have widespread and elaborate campaigns targeted at recruiting a specific consumer: teachers and principals. Even the venture philanthropy groups funding many of these educational companies, such as NewSchools Venture Fund, place emphasis on developing and maintaining their organization's brand (Smith & Peterson, 2006). Educational advocacy organizations are also effective at using marketing to advance their political campaigns. Organizations such as 50Can and Families for Excellent Schools, Inc. run flashy advertising campaigns targeting both political officials and parents.

Finally, private companies have risen to meet the demand of these organizations. Many schools, particularly some of the larger charter management organizations, have glossy marketing campaigns and branded identities built by consultants who have traditionally served private industries, such as consumer packaged goods (CPG) companies, but have begun to tap into this niche of educational marketing (Lamberti, 2014). Today, some marketing firms have created dedicated education "experts" on their teams, and numerous private contractors have built careers around creating materials, such as videos, for educational organizations. For example, the work of Harp Advertising Interactive was critical in developing the marketing campaign and branded identity of the Noble Network in Chicago, including its slogan, "Be Noble" (Harp Advertising website, 2016).

The edvertising industry is a vast, powerful engine, and it is picking up steam.

WHY EDVERTISING?

The reasons for this booming industry are many. At its core, the expansion of market-based policies has directly incentivized the emergence of marketing and branding practices in public education (DiMartino & Jessen, 2014). As Oplatka and Hemsley-Brown (2004) state: "With the market comes marketization" (p. 375). Thus, understanding the evolution of school choice as related to marketing is critical.

Over the years, the infusion of market-based policies into school systems has been touted as a means to various ends: overcoming the persistent inequities of residential segregation in this country, providing competition and stimulation for much-needed reform, or releasing schools from government oversight and bureaucracy, allowing for accountability to parents and students instead. Milton Friedman (1955) advocated for introducing parental choice and market-based competition in the public schools as a means of reform. Contending that if parents were given the opportunity to withdraw from and select schools, "a wide variety of schools would spring up to meet [their] demand." "Competitive enterprise," Friedman wrote, would be a "far more efficient" way of providing quality schooling in the public sector. Yet, despite the long history of choice being put forth as a potential remedy for the nation's ailing public schools, until recently there was not the political or financial support available to create broad-scale choice programs in the public arena.

The publication of *Politics, Markets, and America's Schools* (Chubb & Moe, 1990) hoisted the choice debate into the national spotlight, coinciding with a new political arena that advocated for decreased government involvement, and increased autonomy for school systems in education. The market itself, they argued, would provide oversight for the public schools, removing bureaucratic impediments that, in their opinion, had hindered previous reform efforts.

Chubb and Moe's (1990) ideas about choice were emblematic of a larger-scale political movement toward conservatism and, more particularly, neoliberal and neoconservative ideals (Apple & Pedroni, 2005). This political "conservative alliance" (Apple & Pedroni, 2005) reflected a shifting public faith from the government to the market, and to the private sector in general. Laissez-faire economics, which relied on markets as a policy centerpiece, were espoused widely during the Reagan and first Bush administrations. However, market deregulation was not solely a Republican practice. The emergence and prevalence of neoliberal policies guided the expansion of markets through the next several administrations. The Gramm-Leach-Bliley Act, passed in 1999 by the Clinton administration, exemplified the growing bipartisan faith in market self-regulation, and a simultaneous decline in the belief in the need for government as an external policer. With the neoconservative policies of the second Bush administration, combined with a deep reliance on the private sector, it was clear that the dominant political tenor showed a lack of faith in public institutions.

It is in this era, which Gewirtz (2002) refers to as a "post-welfarist education policy complex" (p. 3), when many policies are based on market competition and operate on Darwinian principles of survival and failure, that the current widespread systems of choice have evolved. In this reform model, "consumers" are, in theory, empowered to select the educational environment that best fits their needs; schools that do not respond to those needs eventually fail and are replaced by better alternatives. For these reasons support for choice policies and charter schools is often framed by a rhetoric of equity or civil rights.

Supporters of markets additionally argue that putting such policies into practice will improve not only the choice schools but the entire public school system (Chubb & Moe, 1990; Friedman, 1955; Greene & Forster, 2002; Hoxby, 2000, 2002). According to the market reform argument, competition for students and funds compels all schools—including nonchoice (usually public) schools—to improve their performance. Without choice, they contend, there is very little incentive to do so (Hoxby, 2000, 2002).

The movement to expand markets to the public educational sector is widespread and diverse in its implementation. At the federal level, a number of recently implemented educational policies have emphasized the role of choice in reform. The No Child Left Behind (NCLB) law provided the "unsafe school choice option," as well as a transfer option when schools consistently failed to meet Adequate Yearly Progress (AYP). Later, the Obama administration's Race to the Top (RttT) as well as i3 grant funding provided financial support for states and districts implementing charter schools and choice programs on larger scales. The Every Student Succeeds Act (2015) continues the public school choice option for failing schools mentioned above, but also adds a new weighted student funding formula (ESSA, 2015). Most recently, the Trump administration has lauded choice policies, and proposed increasing spending to promote vouchers.

Locally, many cities have adopted wide-scale school choice plans. Perhaps most notably, post–Hurricane Katrina New Orleans, where some of our research for this book was conducted, has developed a system of charter schools that currently serves approximately 90% of the student population (Jabbar, 2015; Kamenetz, 2015). New York City uses a complex system of mandatory public high school choice (Jessen, 2011), and numerous other cities, like Philadelphia and Denver, have citywide choice policies of their own.

Choice policies are a direct outgrowth of the increasing role that the private sector and privatization models of reform are playing in public educational systems. Choice policies and, indeed, charter schools and the charter management organizations (CMOs) that oversee many of the charters developed today receive a great deal of support from the private sector. In particular, several foundations funded by successful corporate executives, including, notably, the Bill and Melinda Gates Foundation, the Walton Family Foundation, and the Eli Broad Foundation, have donated vast sums of money to charter development and market policies over the past 15 years. The combined trifecta of financial sanctions from NCLB, the rise of "jurisdictional challengers" such as charter schools, and the flourishing political faith in private sector and market ideals has opened the door for tremendous influence of these three foundations in the public educational arena (Reckhow, 2013).

Over the past 2 decades, we have seen a notable movement of foundation money and policy initiative away from funding innovations associated with traditional public educational institutions or districts and toward charters and their management organizations (Reckhow, 2013). Organizations such as NewSchools Venture Fund, also founded by the business elite, pride themselves on funding public educational "disruptors" who will challenge "the status quo" through markets and innovation (Scott, 2009; Smith & Peterson, 2006). The influence of the Gates Foundation has helped to shape federal policies, such as Race to the Top. The rise to prominence and influence of these "boardroom progressives" (Reckhow, 2013), or the "billionaire boys club" (Ravitch, 2010), has cemented the shift of priorities in the landscape of public education toward private-like agendas—pushing market-based plans, and, simultaneously, as Mr. Fisher noted, promoting the need for national marketing and branding.

By definition, choice policies allow students to select from a portfolio of school options. In order to do so, families must gather information on the available school options, creating the incentive for schools to market themselves to differentiate one school from another as they compete for students (Lubienski, 2007). Getting the message out about the existence of a school, especially a new school or one outside the neighborhood, is a critical piece of educational marketing. These school choice environments are, however, not unregulated markets in the pure economic sense. Rather, they are quasi-markets, as government—federal, state, and local—funds and regulates these public schools (Whitty & Power, 2000).

The organizational and regulatory structure of these markets are murky, as many of these public schools are being founded and managed by privately run charter management organizations. As private-sector entities, CMOs are not held to the same transparency and accountability as their public-sector counterparts. Not only do these management structures push the definition of what constitutes a "public" entity, they make it challenging to collect data on many of their practices, particularly branding and marketing.

In addition, the growth of national organizations and the growing emphasis on franchising, as noted above, necessitate widespread organizational reach and alignment. The entry of a variety of educational management organizations into public education is making marketing more prominent. Unlike most traditional public schools, large or national educational management organizations face a somewhat unique challenge of competing and maintaining their mission in locations and for consumers throughout the country. With schools in multiple cities, and/or teacher recruiting campaigns at colleges around the country, it is in the national management organizations' interest to have cohesive alignment in branding.

Thus, as many organizations have expanded in size, so has the marketing process and competition. As we will see, organizations such as the Success Academy Network, KIPP, and Teach for America bring considerable resources and expertise to the marketing process. These organizations have deeply rooted private-sector networks and/or organizational capacities to support extensive marketing campaigns. Such resources are, arguably, beyond that of their traditional public district or even autonomous charter school counterparts (Jessen & DiMartino, 2016).

This expansion of school and organizational options coupled with the growth of private-sector actors within public education has created a nexus of marketization and educational privatization. These processes have been altered based on educational ideologies and rhetoric, which has moved dialogue and policy away from process and pedagogy, toward outcomes and competition. Within this landscape, we see an embrace of beliefs and practices from the corporate or business world—a shift that directly results in increased branding and marketing practices in public education.

Like the private consumer products industry, educational organizations engage in marketing and branding in order to expand their consumer base. As noted earlier, consumers in public education can be categorized into a few primary groups, including, but not limited to, students and families, teachers, and financial/political supporters. Each of these target audiences can be viewed as a potential "consumer" of the product that the organization is selling. Different organizations may target distinct consumers groups, or multiple ones simultaneously. While CMOs market to attract all three of these groups of consumers, organizations such as Teach for America are primarily targeting teachers, as well as supporters.

The drive to entice teachers and donors are not completely distinct from each other, however. For example, an organization like Teach for America needs to attract teachers in order to make the case to supporters that they are a viable organization that warrants financial investment and political backing. The marketing to teachers and supporters in this case go hand in hand. Maintaining an organizational brand can affect an even broader array of community members, including, for example, the alumni of a school. In examining the activities of edvertising, we should assume that all of these stakeholders have been considered.

In addition, given the intertwined dynamics of large educational organizations and the educational reformers from the corporate sector funding their expansion, the proliferation of marketing practices serves another role—to establish institutional identities for emerging schools or charter networks. Establishing a reputable brand identity and marketing campaign resonates with the venture philanthropy funders. As noted earlier, even organizations that serve as a conduit for money to reach ventures, such as NewSchools Venture Fund, seek to maintain their "brand" in this highly marketized environment (Smith & Peterson, 2006). This identity formation process, in turn, facilitates fundraising from foundations and private donors, potentially further exacerbating inequities. This cycle of fundraising and marketing is often happening beyond the regulation of the public eye, which makes it important to shed light on it.

Edvertising in Practice

Marketing and branding involves many consumer "touch points," as noted by KIPP, including, but not limited to, websites, social media outlets, YouTube channels, press releases, sponsored ads, mailers and fliers, posters, and so on. From typeface to text content, from color-coding to the use of approved stock photos, uniformity in delivering the message of educational institutions has become central to establishing a marketable identity and brand awareness.

These activities come with a price tag, particularly when purchasing services from professional vendors. One of the ways in which large educational organizations support marketing practices is through fundraising from venture philanthropic foundations and their kin, such as the Broad Foundation or NewSchools Venture Fund.

Training has also been developed for smaller or autonomous charter schools to help them compete with larger organizations and target the "right" audiences, while still managing budget limitations. As part of a charter school marketing guide, Brian Carpenter (2014), CEO of the National Charter Schools Institute, explains, "the goal of marketing is to reduce the luck factor by measuring the right things so that you can target the use of your limited resources effectively" (p. 6). It is not surprising, then, that "Digital Marketing 101 for Charter Schools" was a featured presentation at the 2015 National Charter School Conference.

Simply given the rapid and consistent growth of edvertising, educational organizations must find these practices to be a good return on investment. This is likely due in part to their efficacy. Indeed, emerging research has found that parents respond to the increased marketing efforts of schools. DiMartino and Jessen (2014) found that parents were drawn in by branded insignia. Ancess and Allen (2006) found that curricular themes developed by schools are "unspoken codes" that "communicate powerful messages about race, gender, class, income, expectations, college-going, future orientations, definitions of success, and more" (p. 403). The authors assert that students' and parents' responses to these "codes" can potentially result in sorting by ability, socioeconomic status, race, parent involvement, or education levels. Thus, even in developing and promoting curricular themes, schools are engaging in subtle, but powerful, marketing.

Persistent Questions About Edvertising

Despite the rapid growth of the edvertising industry, much of the workings of marketing and branding in public education has, until now, gone unexplored. One of the reasons for this gap in research is due simply to the novelty of these practices. While there exists a wealth of research on marketing in the private sector (consumer products, for example), which we will draw upon in this book, the field of educational research is playing catch-up.

Another reason for the dearth of research is logistical. As mentioned earlier, holding privately managed organizations accountable is difficult because, while they receive public dollars, they are not held to the same reporting requirements as public institutions (DiMartino, 2014; Whitty & Power, 2000). Thus, even when budgets are available, they might not provide detailed, itemized information about marketing practices. Similarly, evaluating the efficacy of marketing messages requires an insider's perspective into these organizations. Because many of the industry leaders are privately managed organizations, this creates a "black box" within schools, or even in the institutions themselves.

Yet examining these practices is critical. Among other things, marketing and branding practices have important implications for equity and access to public education, key educational values and hallmarks of the American education system. The tendency toward increasingly stratified and segregated schools by race, gender, and ability increases in highly marketized environments (Foskett, 2002; Gewirtz, 2002; Hernandez, 2016; Jabbar, 2016b; Lubienski, 2005; Wilson & Carlsen, 2016). Research shows us that the majority of charter school students are low-income students of color; this number increases when examining CMO charter schools or those located in urban centers (National Center for Educational Statistics, 2014). As a result, the practices of edvertising will disproportionately affect these populations. Given the United States' long history of failing to advance educational equity, recognizing the impact of edvertising on low-income communities of color is particularly grave and pressing.

Consumers of all types need keen and critical analytical skills to decipher between the hype and reality of highly cultivated marketing materials. From the perspective of parent and student consumers, this situation gives not only well-educated and English-speaking parents an advantage, but also advantages those who have the time to sift through all of the marketing materials. Research shows that gathering and processing school information is a challenge even for parents with ample time and resources (e.g., see Holme, 2002). A great deal of research is emerging that indicates that schools with a greater degree of marketing resources or capabilities are at an advantage to compete for the best-performing students in an educational marketplace (DiMartino & Jessen, 2014; Jabbar, 2015, 2016b; Jessen & DiMartino, 2016).

As we will see, little research exists on the ways in which teachers or supporters process marketing materials.

THEORETICAL FRAMEWORKS

Given that our book focuses on examining the practice of edvertising at an organizational level, we draw on theories as broad lenses through which to discuss our findings. Because the data on which we draw are diverse in type, we use two primary specific theoretical lenses to frame our analyses: sensemaking and an economic theory of the value of goods. While the former provides a framework with which to interpret the behavior of the actors imbedded in organizations, the latter provides a perspective on the organizations as a whole.

Sensemaking Theory

The concept of sensemaking provides a useful framework for interpreting the actions and experiences of the key actors involved with edvertising. Sensemaking allows us to reflect on how parents, teachers, students, principals, marketing directors, and media salespeople construct meaning around their identities, organizations, practices, and experiences within these highly marketized educational settings.

Sensemaking is, as Weick (1995) states, "that act of making sense" (p. 4). Specifically, sensemaking investigates how meaning is constructed, why it is constructed, by whom, and with what impacts. According to Weick, seven key properties of sensemaking make it distinct from other explanatory processes. Sensemaking is (1) grounded in identity construction; (2) retrospective; (3) enactive of sensible environments; (4) social; (5) outgoing; (6) focused on extracted cues; and (7) driven by plausibility rather than accuracy. Below we will describe these seven properties and apply them to our work with edvertising.

Property 1. "Grounded in identity construction" speaks to how people see themselves as individuals but also as actors within the larger organization in which they work. Such grounding links individuals' self-perception with others' perception of them as individuals but also as members of a larger collective. This speaks directly to our study of edvertising. For example, many national CMOs create brand manuals for their schools. Principals, teachers, and students have to follow the key branding tenets of the organization as outlined by the manual, such as what colors their uniforms should be and how to discuss their school with the media. Here, school-level actors must make sense of their organization's brand for themselves—as teachers, learners, leaders, and, of course, as citizens—but also make sense of what being affiliated with such a brand means. Specifically, what does this brand affiliation mean for them as actors within the brand but also as representatives of it? How will outsiders perceive them?

Property 2. "Retrospective" relates to the idea that we can truly know what happened only after we have lived the experience. Here, meaning-making is a process that takes place over an extended period of time. This property also speaks to the power of context, as viewed through an historical lens, to explain how and why organizations act as they do. District and school leaders, who are immersed in building their organization's brand, are deep in the enactment mode, creating their visual signifiers and contracting with advertising firms to get their message out. These actors will be able to truly understand what they are constructing and the implications of it only after their campaigns are complete. A poignant example of retrospective surfaced when we interviewed a videographer who made high-gloss pro-charter videos for Success Academy Charter Schools. During the interview, she shared that while creating the videos, she felt she was simply doing her job. She didn't realize until postproduction, when she had a child in a traditional public school, that in fact her pro-charter advocacy work for Success Academy did not fit with her deep commitment to public education. This level of sensemaking could occur only after the fact, when she had the time and space to fully interpret her actions and accompanying sentiments.

Property 3. "Enactive of sensible environments" relates to the idea that actors actively construct their realities through their actions, such as enacting laws or making an advertisement that didn't previously exist. Or, as Weick (1995) says, "people create their environments as those environments create them" (p. 34). This idea helps us understand the responses of teachers in areas of intense school choice competition.

Property 4. "Social" implies that sensemaking is a shared activity, contingent on the interactions of all players. When discussing edvertising "social" speaks to the messages embedded in the ad campaigns themselves and, further, the meaning-making that occurs between the ad itself and the people who consume it.

Property 5. "Ongoing" suggests that sensemaking never ends; it is a process that continues as meaning is continually being constructed and enacted. To this end, all participants in these highly competitive school choice environments are continuously constructing and enacting their lived experiences, which in turn are reshaping traditional conceptions of public education.

Property 6. "Focused on extracted cues" means that sensemaking is about interpretation and that contextual cues can promote understanding. Here the idea is that even small or subtle cues can influence sensemaking, and further, that active sensemaking means allowing the cues to continuously update one's own interpretive processes. Cues, in many ways, are the cornerstone of edvertising. It's the cues that can shape personal beliefs and opinions about particular schools, which directly affects school choice.

Property 7. "Driven by plausibility rather than accuracy" indicates that, in sensemaking, essence is enough—accurate perception is not a necessity. According to Weick (1995), it is belief rather than accuracy that guides action. Campaigns that promise college acceptance or even access to Ivy League institutions speak to parents' desire and belief in their children, but they might not be an accurate representation of what the school can actually deliver. Here, schools might be making claims about higher education attainment that have yet to actually bear out. For example, a school might brand itself as college preparatory without having any graduates yet enrolled in college. Parents choose a school based on their belief in a school's plausible claims—even if the claims are not supported by evidence.

Economic Value of Goods

In addition to sensemaking, we use an economic principle to frame some of our analysis. This principle is called the subjective theory of values or goods (Menger, 1976). Menger's reconceptualization of the value of goods was that the perceived value of a good was subjective in nature—that value was placed on the good based on the perception or desires of the consumer. Marketing is, in effect, entirely an arena revolving around conveying (or creating) the subjective value of goods in order to attract consumers. In public education, this theory of values has a unique context, in that very few people would say that education has no value in and of itself. Hence, when marketing educational institutions, it becomes necessary for organizations or schools to convey their value as distinguishably *more valuable* than other organizations or schools on the market. This is where the quality and content of marketing and branding materials becomes an essential conveyer of value.

Economic theory also outlines the concept of "experienced goods." In marketing research, a product is deemed valued by consumers if it is repeatedly purchased. Experienced goods are products or services whose value is understood once the experience is completed. Schooling is such a good (Buckley & Schneider, 2007). Evaluating the experience of a school might not be possible until one has long since graduated. One can argue that it is hard to perceive the value of education until well into adult life. In addition, public schooling is not something that can be re-purchased.

Additional layers of complexity about the role of school marketing in a consumer goods model can be raised based on who is doing the choosing. Asymmetries in information, as communicated through marketing campaigns, can significantly influence choice outcomes. In addition, questions can be raised about whether consumers can have a clear understanding of the outcomes of selecting certain schools given that they, themselves, do not attend the schools. Duarte and Hastings (2012) discuss how in situations in which the one choosing the "good" (i.e., product or service) does not experience the good as part of the choosing process, that person must rely on other *indicators* to judge its value. They write that the phenomenon of people making decisions using what they call "suboptimal information," relying primarily on marketing or branding, "calls into question the extent to which increased choice and privatization can lead to increased efficiency in traditionally publically provided markets like social security, education, and health care" (p. 2).

This is where marketing and branding become centrally important in educational settings—conveying the value of a school or organization to parents or teachers who cannot immediately or directly experience the good themselves.

ABOUT THIS BOOK

As we have seen, the advertising world is rapidly expanding, powerful in its impact in public education, yet little explored and operating outside of the public eye. It is within this arena that we seek to shed light.

This book explores multiple components of the complex dynamics of edvertising in public education today. Throughout, we examine the role of edvertising from an organizational perspective. Our focus is on the marketing practices of the organizations, as well as the perspectives on these practices of actors who are imbedded within these organizations, including marketing executives and teachers. Specifically, our book captures the landscape of edvertising across key organizational fields within public education, including leadership and governance, budgeting and finance, strategic initiatives, the use and impact of new technologies, the role of organizational actors (including teachers), and the organizational messaging itself. In approaching our analysis from an organizational perspective, we acknowledge that, many times, these organizations are driving and shaping the landscape of public education.

In addition, our book examines the ethical tensions that emerge as a result of edvertising practices. Broadly, we review the questions and potential unintended outcomes of such practices that need to be addressed by the educational community. Simply distributing information is different from fundraised, glossified, targeted campaigns conducted with the goal of competing to expand consumer base or build the power and scope of the parent organization. Marketing is one piece of a larger shift within the realm of public education policies toward business-oriented practices and privatization. This book ultimately raises questions about the virtues of such aims, which, we contend, can run contrary to civic, democratic, and equitable purposes of public education. Public education is one of the United States' largest institutions of democracy, so understanding and evaluating marketing and branding within this realm is essential.

We begin laying a foundation in Chapter 1, "What We Know About Edvertising: Marketing, Branding, and Advertising in Public Education" which provides a comprehensive groundwork for the rest of the book. By integrating research from business and education, we show how approaches long embraced by the private sector are being co-opted by the public sector. In this chapter, we present the seminal research studies in the field and also highlight key gaps in the literature that the research presented in this book fills.

In Chapters 2 through 4, we outline what the edvertising industry looks like today from an organizational perspective. In Chapter 2, "Edumarketers: The Emergence of a New Executive Class in Public Education," we introduce the new roles created as a result of the emergence of edvertising. Drawing on interviews with key educational marketing executives, we explore how the position "director of marketing" has become an organizational norm. We explore these new actors' roles and responsibilities, as well as examine the costs associated with the salaries of these positions. We also identify key market leaders in the field and reflect on how their efforts affect schools less engaged in the practice of image management. In Chapter 3,

"'An Expression of Values': Four Case Studies of Edvertising Budgets," we examine the money spent on marketing. This chapter provides an in-depth analysis of the cost of edvertising. By analyzing school-level budgets from four regions—New Orleans; Washington, DC; New York; and Massachusetts—this chapter sheds light into the proverbial "black box" around the cost of edvertising. In Chapter 4, "The Activities of Edvertising: Traditional and Digital Advertisements," we provide a comprehensive description of the branding and marketing practices used by the district central office, charter management organizations, and schools in New York City. From traditional print to online advertising, this section provides data on advertising procedures, costs, and reach.

In Chapters 5 through 7, we examine how organizations construct and interpret marketing in education. In Chapter 5, "Perceptions of Prestige: An Analysis of Digital Marketing," we look at how schools in the Boston and New York City metro areas engage in digital and social media marketing and branding. Chapter 6, "Becoming the Organization: Teachers as Edvertising Actors," takes us to New Orleans, where we hear from teachers working within one of the most marketized educational environments in the United States. We learn from teachers how they make sense of their multiple roles within various organizations—including Teach for America, charter networks, and schools. We document how teachers negotiate their positions as consumers, educators, and—sometimes—even as ambassadors of brands.

In Chapter 7, "Net Impressions: Where Rhetoric Meets Reality," we dive into an exploration of some of the specific claims of edvertising. The private-sector advertising industry has long struggled with how to ensure that companies' claims align with the reality of their product. Government agencies exist to regulate such advertising, and the private sector itself has set up commissions to self-regulate its advertisements. But what happens in education? Drawing on discourse analysis of multiple marketing videos as well as the New Orleans teacher data, this chapter sheds light on this question.

We conclude with a discussion of broad implications and findings in Chapter 8, "Conclusion: The Future of Edvertising." In this chapter we provide recommendations for the edvertising industry as it marches forward.

CHAPTER 1

What We Know About Edvertising

Marketing, Branding, and Advertising in Public Education

The proliferation of increased and varied edvertising practices across the K–12 sector has outpaced the research. Only a handful of scholars have made headway into the practices and outcomes of educational marketing. In addition, while there is a substantial pool of academic research on marketing, branding, and advertising coming from academic research in business schools, the connections between those studies as applied to educational settings have not been frequently made. A review of the business literature raises important questions about how educational consumers might experience different brands and their related marketing campaigns.

To provide a basis for further discussion, this chapter reviews the existing research on several topics. Primarily, we outline research both from the fields of business and education, and create connections between them to further our understanding of edvertising practices.

ON MARKETING, BRANDING, AND ADVERTISING: CONNECTING BUSINESS TO EDUCATIONAL RESEARCH

While in public education, marketing, branding, and advertising are relatively new activities, in the private sector they are longstanding practices. As such, there exists a wealth of academic research in these arenas. In this section, we review some key components within this field.

Building a Brand

Silk (2006) outlines a number of vehicles through which value can be delivered, including "the physical product itself," "brand name," "company reputation," "convenience availability," and "word-of-mouth references from earlier adopter of the product" (p. 10). In the educational world, similar channels exist, with critical differences. First, since there is not one concrete definition of *product* in education, we address two types of ways of translating value through the "physical product itself." The physical product could be considered to be the appearance of the school and affiliated imagery—the school, building, uniforms, students, classroom facilities, or, in lieu of actual contact with a physical building, simply a school's use of images. Even the school's neighborhood can be lumped into the overall image of product. The powerful influence images and impressions of the physical product have on parents' and students' choices has been well documented in the literature on education (Cucchiara, 2013; DiMartino & Jessen, 2014; Jabbar, 2016a, 2016b; Lubienski, 2007).

To a degree, a school's reputation or, in the parlance of the business world, "company reputation," has always been a crucial part of the public educational system. Company reputation is closely linked with branded identity, and the equity of a brand. By definition, branding is one component of an overall marketing agenda. Many of us are familiar with a variety of brands, including the Nike swoosh symbol and the McDonald's arches. Brands are "names or symbols that marketers have introduced to make product differentiation concrete . . . [and] different from those offered by competitors" (Silk, 2006, p. 100). In its simplest form, brands are visual signifiers of a particular product or company.

Conducting a branding exercise is often the first step in the process of marketing a school or organization. As Foskett (2002) shared, "Marketing may be seen as an operational process, involving, for example, promotional, sales and public relationship activities. Alternatively, it may be regarded as a holistic approach to the management of an organization which encompasses its mission, strategies and operations" (p. 245). When starting with a well-defined school mission, the "how" and "to whom" that mission is communicated becomes a question of operational tactics. In fact, it can be argued that a positive outcome of interschool and district competition is in influencing organizations to go through the exercise of defining a school mission in order to distinguish their brand from those of others (Foskett, 2002; Harvey, 1996; James & Phillips, 1995).

This mission-building exercise is not the sole provenance of school leaders and administrators; parents can get in on the act, too. In a recent study, Olson Beal and Beal (2016) highlight the growth of "brand communities." In this study, parents in particular became intimately involved with supporting and promoting a school's brand. Buy-in was so strong, in fact, that their involvement moved beyond simple image production and into a perceived culture of exclusivity. Parents perceived their brand as being a "good fit" for some families, but not others (p. 93).

While a certain theory of branding argues that advertising materials should reflect a carefully considered organizational mission, research has also found that brand-building often focuses on "glossification" or "impression management": attention to the look and feel of a brand, but not actual information about the brand itself (Adnett & Davies, 2005; Gewirtz, Ball, & Bowe, 1995; Lubienski, 2005; Symes, 1998). Gewirtz and colleagues

(1995) found that schools in England built their brands by adopting "corporate colors" (p. 128) and school logos and symbols, rather than by focusing on curricular or pedagogical improvements. Studies have also found that in high-choice district environments, schools tend to cluster around particular themes, such as college preparation, and use similar language, such as academy and scholar (DiMartino & Jessen, 2014; Lubienski & Lee, 2016). Likewise, Lubienski and Lee's (2016) examination of charter school mission statements across schools in Detroit were very similar, focusing on a theme of academics rather than life-learning, citizenship, or diversity. These findings led researchers to question whether, if all of the brands were similar, there really was much "choice," practically speaking, in the reality of school choice.

Branding can also relate to the assessment of the physical product, particularly when discussing evaluating school facilities or other visual indicators. Developing a clear visually branded "campus" identity is a popular trend, not just for charter schools, but also for many schools as they are just opening—particularly if they are co-locating in a building, for example (Rubin, 2004).

Reaching the Consumer

Continuing with Silk's (2006) categories, the concept of marketing or sharing information about schools via word of mouth has been discussed numerous times in the school choice literature. In the field of education, many researchers have concluded that rather than being based on performance-based "rationality" in an economic sense, parents' educational decisionmaking is often a social process shaped by networks of relationships (Andre-Bechely, 2005; Ball, 2007; Bell, 2009; Bosetti, 2004; Cucchiara, 2013; Gewirtz et al., 1995; Holme, 2002). Research shows that parents rely heavily on their social networks when making educational choices (Bell, 2009; Kimelberg & Billingham, 2013; Oplatka, 2007). Oplatka's (2007) study of Canadian parents, teachers, and students' perceptions of the school choice process found that proximity to home, friends, and word of mouth were more influential than an open house or school fair. Similarly, both Bell (2009) and Kimelberg and Billingham's (2013) studies of school choice showed that parents relied on their own peer networks to exchange ideas about and gather information on different schooling options.

Due to the power of social networks, educational organizations spend resources on marketing practices not just to influence the immediate impressions of those who take in a particular advertisement, but also their friends and neighbors. As we will see, many CMOs lead "community outreach" events that serve as both a specific recruiting opportunity and community brand-building.

According to emerging research, in addition to their endeavors on the ground CMOs, educational organizations, districts, and schools are using an increasingly wide array of media to market themselves (Cucchiara, 2013; DiMartino & Jessen, 2014; Hernandez, 2016; Jabbar, 2016a; Jessen & DiMartino, 2016; Lubienski, 2005; Symes, 1998; Wilkins, 2012; Wilson & Carlsen, 2016). No longer confined to fliers, brochures, and school fairs, marketing takes place across the breadth of modern media channels, from traditional media outlets such as radio, billboard, and newspapers to digital and social media. Recent studies have begun to capture the use of digital marketing practices in public education (Drew, 2013; Hernandez, 2016; Jessen & DiMartino, 2016; Wilkins, 2012; Wilson & Carlsen, 2016).

CMOs, in particular, are frontrunners in using digital media to advertise their schools. Jessen and DiMartino's (2016) study found that CMOs were the leaders in creating well-crafted social media campaigns. Using channels like YouTube and Twitter, CMOs hired professional videographers and photographers to fill the content on their social media sites, which stood in stark contrast to the homemade videos often found on traditional public school and autonomous charter school websites. Additional studies found that the placement of pictures and images, as well as language used on school websites, was carefully orchestrated to target particular communities (Cucchiara, 2013; Hernandez, 2016; Wilkins, 2012; Wilson & Carlsen, 2016).

MARKET LEADERS, CHALLENGERS, FOLLOWERS, AND NICHERS

Within any field, some product companies are dominant, with a broad, strong consumer base. These products or product companies are known as the "market leaders." Trailing the market leaders, and trying to extract some of their consumer base, are several categories of competitors. According to Cueller-Healey and Gomez (2013), "The roles played by firms in an industry can be usefully classified into: market leader, market challenger, market follower, or market nicher." Market challengers actively attack the market leader via a variety of strategies in an attempt to siphon off consumers to sustain their own business. This could mean, for example, portraying the market leader at failing to serve customers. Market followers, on the other hand, engage in competition with market leaders by "copy[ing] some things from the leader but maintain[ing] some differentiation in packaging, advertising, pricing, etc." (Cueller-Healey & Gomez, 2013, p. 14). They do not directly attack the market leader because it is not in their interest to do so. Finally, market nichers develop a unique product specialization—often targeting a smaller market than the leader (say, for example, a local region).

In education, one can point to the public educational system as the market leader, and the variety of "jurisdictional challengers" (Reckhow, 2013) as the contenders in the market based on the many rhetorical and political campaigns to discredit the public educationl system. However, as the landscape of schools of choice and privately managed educational organizations have expanded, they have developed leaders and challengers within their own ranks.

PRODUCT POSITIONING AND MARKET SEGMENTATION

Product positioning is a key component of marketing, which involves crafting a message that reaches a specific target market (Silk, 2006). The concept of market segmentation and product differentiation was originally put forward by Smith (1956), who contended that marketing should be tailored to specific groups of people. Through segmentation, customers are divided into generalized groups with assumed similar preferences (e.g., "millennials" or "mothers"). Marketing campaigns are then targeted to those particular groups—called product differentiation—based on a common understanding of their interests and values.

With respect to public education, and most particularly charter schools, segmentation and product differentiation plays an interesting role. The vast majority of students are served by the public educational system. Charter schools make up about 6% of the public schools in the country. However, a disproportionate amount (56%) of students enrolled in charter schools are located in urban areas, while students living in urban areas account for only 29% of the overall population, according to Mead, Mitchell, and Rotherham (2015). This number becomes even more skewed when looking at the locations of major CMO chains around the country, which predominantly locate in low-income urban areas. With the notable exception of having access to online charter schools, suburban and rural charter student enrollment tends to be much lower, and is predominantly found in autonomous schools.

Examining this phenomenon from a market segmentation perspective, we argue that, for a variety of reasons, the charter school market is already strategically segmented for the marketing purposes. For example, broadly, markets in public education are segmented by geographic region. By necessity, schools in Los Angeles are not competing with schools in Boston. Rural schools are less frequently able to access schools beyond local, traditional public schools, which is in part why virtual schooling has targeted this segment of the U.S. student population. Thus, each geographic region represents a type of segmentation.

Edvertising activities typically target a particular set, or market segment, of consumers. In the best-case scenario, this is so the most relevant message is reaching the "right" audience—in this case, parents and students—who are likely to be interested in a school/organization's particular theme. Teachers, as we will see later, represent a different market segment from parents.

However, the concerning corollary to this is the potentially inequitable sorting of students into schools. With high-stakes standardized testing policies, schools can be tempted to target marketing campaigns at a higher-achieving student set. Thus, marketing can accelerate stratification between schools and even contribute to the resegregation of public schools (Foskett, 2002; Gewirtz, 2002; Gewirtz et al., 1995; Hernandez, 2016; Jabbar, 2016b; Lubienski, 2005; Wilson & Carlsen, 2016).

Along the same lines, targeted marketing campaigns from schools have been seen as having been positioned to intentionally weed out higher-needs students (Jennings, 2010; Jessen, 2013) or to project an elite image to attract a population of higher-achieving students and their parents (Drew, 2013; Hernandez, 2016; Jabbar, 2016a). Hernandez (2016) examined web-based marketing materials from two CMOs and found the CMOs negatively portraying the Black and Latino communities that they served, in order to show how their schools would reverse the "negative patterns" of poverty and low achievement in the surrounding communities (p. 48). In doing this, Hernandez argued, these organizations avoided active discussions of race and rather used insinuating images and assertions to attract parents.

In market theory, this is part of the selection game—some producers reach their target audience more effectively than others. In the compulsory public educational system, targeted marketing campaigns, making potentially exaggerated or erroneous claims, and shifting educational resources toward marketing have the potential to erode the fundamental democratic principles of public education.

CONSUMER PREFERENCES

Business literature has long examined the effects of advertising and marketing in shaping consumer preferences. Marshall (1919) distinguished between "constructive" advertising, which primarily relayed information to the consumer, and "combative" marketing, which focused on saturating a market with a brand or marketing campaign. Later on, models were developed to examine the ways in which companies create widespread market knowledge about their new products (Butters, 1977).

There are several prominent and longstanding theories about how advertising and marketing campaigns signal product value to consumers, particularly in instances where the product is an *experienced* good (rather than, say, a tangible product that can be possessed), such as education. Milgrom and Roberts (1986) argue that in the case of experienced goods, advertising and marketing are used implicitly to signal to the consumer the quality of the product. They argue that among these "signals" is simply that the perceived amount of money being spent on the advertisement or marketing campaign is enough to communicate to consumers that the product itself is of high quality. Galbraith (1976) argued, similarly, that advertising in and of itself can convey prestige. Ackerberg (2001) adds that "firms signal better quality or taste with high levels of advertising expenditures" (p. 319).

Becker and Murphy (1993) contend that part of the reason for this effect is that consumers want to associate themselves with particular brands, or highly recognized ones. In addition, researchers have argued that the more frequently consumers see an ad for a particular product, the more likely they are to subconsciously assume that a great degree of money has been spent on that product. Therefore, frequency of contact with an ad or marketing campaign translates to perceptions of quality (Nelson, 1974).

More recently, research indicates that businesses have begun to attempt to shape consumer preferences rather than adapting to consumer demand. According to Dawar (2013):

> But the reality is that companies are increasingly finding success not by being responsive to customers' stated preferences but by defining what customers are looking for and shaping their "criteria of purchase." When asked about the market research that went into the development of the iPad, Steve Jobs famously replied, "None. It's not the consumers' job to know what they want."

Ironically, this type of shaping conflicts with the essential components of market competition, but aligns with marketing strategy: rather than follow consumer preferences, convince consumers via marketing what products they want or need. We return to this issue in the final chapters of this book.

As noted earlier, according to Silk (2006), marketing is "the process via which a firm creates value for its chosen customers. Value is created by meeting customer needs" (p. 3). Creating value is a key component of any marketing plan. In the case of "experienced goods," such as schools, where the product is only known after some time, marketing becomes central to establishing a product value.

Research on parents' experiences with educational marketing is limited. Some research examines parental participation in school-level branding and marketing efforts, usually through involvement in parent–teacher associations (Cucchiara, 2013; Olson Beal & Beal, 2016). Olson Beal and Beal's (2016) case study of a school in a high-choice environment found that parents were deeply involved in school-level branding and marketing activities. Efforts included setting up public relations events for schools, assigning groups of parents to street outreach, and recruiting parents who are marketing or creative professionals to donate their talents to the school's marketing campaign. A key finding from this study is that the social and political capital of middle- and upper-middle-class families gives them a clear advantage when it comes to promoting schools (Olson Beal & Beal, 2016). Similarly, Cucchiara (2013) and Posey-Maddox's (2014) research on parental behavior within school choice landscapes found that middle- and upper-middle-class families were at an advantage in terms of supporting, advocating for and promoting their schools as compared to less advantaged parents. Since most school choice occurs in urban settings, which are often segregated by race and class, these findings have serious implications for building and sustaining equitable school systems.

There is scant research on parents' and students' perceptions of their decision in highly marketized environments. DiMartino and Jessen's (2014) study of small schools is one of the few studies to look at how parents and students make sense of how individual schools' marketing messages match the reality of their school environments. In this study, researchers found that the hype often did not match the reality. A study by Stewart and Good (2016) also examined how parents choose between after-school providers amidst much marketing noise. A key finding from this study was that parents lacked information from an objective, trusted actor about their school choices. Additionally, these researchers called for moderate oversight of marketing practices.

EDVERTISING RESOURCES: TIME AND MONEY

As indicated by Ackerberg (2001), advertising requires a significant amount of resources—both time and money. Research shows that an emphasis on branding and marketing potentially changes the traditional roles educators' play. At the principal level, more focus is turned externally toward image management, and away from internal school issues (Anderson, 2009; Jabbar, 2015; Olson Beal & Beal, 2016; Oplatka, 2002). For teachers, their approach in the classroom can become circumscribed by the delivery of a branded model of education, allowing less room for personalization of teaching practices (Foskett, 2002; Jessen, 2011; Oplatka, 2006). Chapters 6 and 7 in this book speak directly to the experiences of teachers working in New Orleans, one of the most competitive school choice environments in the United States.

With an increased emphasis on marketing and branding, schools are diverting time and financial resources into navigating educational markets with marketing campaigns. Allocating a greater proportion of school finances toward marketing practices might leave less for programmatic uses (Jessen, 2011; Lubienski, 2005; Olson Beal & Beal, 2016). Such shifts in budgets are often justified with the belief that marketing will yield increases in student applications and enrollment, and subsequent tuition dollars to follow (Jabbar, 2015; Olson Beal & Beal, 2016). For CMO-run charter schools, the ability to raise money to contribute to expansive and glossified marketing campaigns can put public schools—both traditional and autonomous charter—at a disadvantage (Hernandez, 2016; Jennings, 2010; Wilson & Carlsen, 2016).

A few studies discuss monetary allotments to marketing, specifically. In general, the literature here is lacking, primarily because quantitative data are mostly nonexistent. Some research draws on qualitative statements about marketing expenditures, indicating that, for educational leaders, the decision to invest in marketing is wrapped up in the overall budget, potentially involving problematic trade-offs for tightening budgets. Jessen (2011) found that small schools competing in mandatory high school choice in New York City have to allocate money from the school budget to engage in required marketing activities. One principal of a small school discussed these trade-offs:

> We use our regular budget [to market]. The first four years, you
> know, we had the New Visions grant. The startup grant from the
> Gates Foundation. We used that. . . . [Now] we have to use the school
> money for it. We do what we've got to. I have to pay teachers to stay
> late for open houses, I choose to do that. I do what I have to do.

This principal indicated that, initially, marketing efforts were supported by philanthropic investments from the Gates Foundation. However, once that grant funding ended, the school had to reallocate money for marketing to support their marketing endeavors.

Similarly, in a study of a local education market in Michigan, Lubienski (2007) found that charter schools tended to use emotional appeals to attract parents. At open houses and in brochures, parents hear about safety, discipline, facilities, and activities, but were rarely presented with information on school effectiveness. He raised concerns that funds for marketing and recruiting practices were detracting from the academic budget and focus of schools in the marketplace. In particular, events such as open houses and fairs, which typically require unionized staff members to work overtime, can quickly become expensive endeavors.

Lack of transparency around financial investments, in marketing, recruiting, branding, and advertising, is a pervasive theme in the literature. In the few studies that have specifically tried to unearth budgets for educational marketing, there has been little success. In a New Orleans–based study, Fottrell and colleagues (2015) examined radio station and bus stop ads for charter school marketing. By canvassing the city, they found that many major network-affiliated charter schools, including KIPP and ReNEW, were purchasing ads specifically targeting certain neighborhoods. As part of this study, they examined budgets to assess the financial investment behind these campaigns. They found that most schools do not provide itemized budgets, particularly in the Recovery School District. They conclude by arguing that "budgets should be continually posted and have standard, required categories for itemization, including advertising expenses" (Fottrell et al., 2015, p. 3).

As this chapter has revealed, findings from the literature illustrate the need for more research on branding and marketing practices in public education. Our book fills this gap across key research areas by adding our new data on district officials' roles in edvertising, the intricacies of marketing budgets, and the actual cost of marketing, as well as on the net impressions experienced across a variety of consumers, including teachers and parents. By examining the expansion, cost, and organizational impact of branding and marketing on schools, we shine a light on this direct consequence of market-based education reforms.

CHAPTER 2

Edumarketers

The Emergence of a New Executive Class in Public Education

In our examination of edvertising across multiple organizational fields within public education, it is appropriate to begin our discussion by turning to those who construct the edvertising industry: leadership and governance.

As Chapter 1 documented, edvertising practices in public education have become more common. To date, much of the research on actors in this system has focused on the role that individual school leaders play in marketing schools (Jabbar, 2015; Oplatka, 2007). This chapter examines the new leaders in the field: the district management or CMO leaders involved in the strategic decisionmaking around branding and marketing. We argue that as schools and management organizations focus on building a strong brand across multiple institutions on a broader scale, locally and nationally, the overarching management organization becomes more critical in driving the marketing agenda.

Because of this new organizational focus on marketing, it is common to find executives with titles such as vice president of marketing and communications or director of digital communication working at charter management companies, whose job it is to manage marketing and branding of the organization. More recently, such roles have been created in the central offices of public districts. The emergence of these generally high-paying executive roles marks a shift in the institutional landscape of public education. Understanding these pivotal roles is critical given the demonstrated importance of marketing and branding of education in conveying quality to consumers, the concerns raised about shifting organizational purpose and educational budgets toward paying for endeavors such as marketing (Jessen, 2011; Lubienski, 2005), as well as the potential for inequitable targeting of certain populations via marketing (Hernandez, 2016; Wilson & Carlsen, 2016).

This chapter examines the roles, responsibilities, and compensation of these newest additions to the educational arena—educational marketing executives in New York City. We not only categorize the individual roles themselves, but also begin to classify the organizations in which they work, vis-à-vis their strategic power and background in marketing and institutional trajectory toward engaging in the market in this manner.

We use case study methodology (Stake, 1995) to explore the roles, responsibilities, and salaries of marketing and communications personnel in the highly competitive educational marketplace of New York City. We chose to focus on New York City because of its established system of school choice and the variety of organizational and educational options, including charter schools, small schools, and traditional zoned options (Bulkley, Henig, & Levin, 2010). Through interviews with marketing and communications personnel at CMOs and at the New York City Department of Education (NYC DOE), as well as reviews of IRS 990 forms and state websites that offer public use data on employees, we gathered information about the work, experiences, and compensation of individuals in charge of marketing and branding in public education. This allowed us to build a clearer understanding of the evolution of the educational landscape.

It is important to document that while the NYC DOE and many CMOs were willing participants, some CMOs were not. In terms of process, we contacted, via email or phone, over 30 New York City–based marketing and communications professionals. While some potential participants responded quickly and readily agreed to be interviewed, some organizations, most notably Success Academy, refused to participate in the study. For example, we sent over 20 queries to multiple individuals within the Success Academy network, and none of the individuals consented to be interviewed. Additionally, when probed about budget and salary, many of the officials—at both the school district and the CMO—would not provide exact details. In order to gain more specific financial data discussed in Chapter 3, we interviewed the providers—advertising firms, for example—to find out their fee structures. While we actively pursued this data, the lack of transparency and access to some organizations is a limitation of this study.

In total, we interviewed 16 district management and CMO personnel or advertising executives. The organizations represented in this sample constitute the majority of the players in the educational management field in the city—with the notable exception of Success Academy.

THE EVOLUTION OF THE EDUCATIONAL
MARKETING INDUSTRY IN NEW YORK CITY

We found that a significant organizational shift within the educational landscape of New York City occurred over the past decade toward competition through the institutional prioritization of marketing efforts. The growth of the role of marketing executives is emblematic of, and central to, this shift.

The Race to Market: Building Organizational Capacity

While forms of marketing and choice have existed for nearly 2 decades in New York City, Bloomberg and Klein's 2006 portfolio school model marks the beginning of a sprint to expand educational marketing and branding. The district management, CMOs, and schools began responding incrementally. At the district and CMO level, media and communications offices housed the early marketing staff. In the early days, especially among CMOs—which were nascent themselves—the majority of the branding work was done pro bono (for the public good) by advertising agencies.

In this early era, the position of director of marketing (or similar) was new to many organizations. The director of marketing at a national CMO shared her initial experiences at the organization: "[B]efore I came to [CMO], there was no director of marketing. I don't think anyone was thinking about branding." She continued, "for example, we have 49 schools and a lot of our schools, they don't use the same naming convention!" This quotation captures the ambiguity within organizations as they transformed themselves to become more competitive in the educational marketplace. Individuals had to re-imagine their roles and responsibilities within organizations.

According to our interviews, in New York City, the 2013–2014 academic year roughly marks an intensive institutional shift toward educational competition, and, in response, the revving up of the educational marketing industry. An executive at a leading private marketing firm in New York City, which today provides graphic design, printing, and direct-mail services for the NYC DOE and CMOs, best notes this change:

> It started out maybe it was like 20 schools [in 2010], and then the word got out, and people were calling me the following year, now I work with at least 50. . . . It's been very interesting because initially I handled the work by myself, and then 2 or 3 years into it I was getting a little crazy, and I wound up having to have someone else work with me. There's lots more charter schools now. They compete with each other. . . . They are all trying to appeal to a certain group.

This executive raises several interesting points. First, she clearly highlights the institutional shifts toward prioritizing marketing throughout the city at a variety of educational institutions. She also indicates that the charter and CMO business is driving the competitive landscape and, in effect, creating the educational marketing industry. These marketing campaigns also have a targeted population "trying to appeal to a certain group" within their messaging.

While district management and CMOs often work with marketing firms such as the one described above, they have also built up their own in-house capacity over the past years. All participants reported that internal capacity building occurred around this time to further integrate a vision for branding and marketing into their organizations. This became especially important for two reasons: (1) The local NYC educational landscape became increasingly competitive. Organizations responded to this increased competition by working to further differentiate their brand from their peers and by increasing their advertising efforts. And, (2) some charter management organizations were scaling up nationally and as a result were spending resources on growing their national brand. A current director of marketing at a leading national CMO described this time of transition:

> There was not a communications function of the department. I think they used an external firm for any communications needs. With my position it became the marketing and communications department, [and] at that point we were working with a couple of freelancers. Now when I was given the task of leading the department, I was asked what do we think the future is. I think the future is not just making signs for schools, but being able to advise on how to market ourselves in a way that I think we haven't had to. As the landscape is getting even more competitive, we really have to differentiate ourselves. For that reason, I think we were able to get a creative director in house. Moving the design function in-house was honestly a cost saving thing as well. If you're not having to seek out and pay freelancers for each project, it's a good cost savings.

Creating in-house marketing teams, according to this interviewee, is distinct from having a communications department, in that marketing is inherently more proactively engaged in shaping the organization's success in the competitive landscape. Here, again, we see the strategic decision to create this role and department directly in response to competition: "[T]he landscape is getting . . . more competitive." Additionally, budget-wise, it is more cost effective and efficient to have on-staff graphic designers or social media managers than to pay for independent consultants.

In our interviews and research, we found many CMOs have multi-person marketing teams working in-house today. While variation exists across organizations, the in-house teams tend to consist of marketing executives, graphic designers, copywriters, and communications managers for digital media and social media platforms. As one director of marketing at a national CMO described, "we are a full-service team that handles all manner of marketing, branding, communications for the organization." In this example, and in the quote above, we see the transition of branding and marketing from being ad hoc and outsourced to being an integral part of these organizations' institutional fabric. The development of these teams is an investment in the implementation of these organizations' strategic visions to spread their brand and firmly establish themselves within the educational marketplace.

In response to the competition during this era, New York City's public district began to take note. No longer was the role of "director of marketing" limited to CMOs; the New York City Department of Education opened its marketing office in 2012. An official at the NYC DOE described the extent to which they actively shape their branded identity: "Those logos were designed years ago by City Hall. So we've inherited those. But all the other work that we do to the large extent we design in-house. Again, occasionally we may hire an ad agency or an outside firm." Much of the work of the NYC DOE marketing office appears to be reacting to trends being led by CMOs and charters, even though, as discussed later, marketing officials at the NYC DOE report that they generally do not feel threatened by the expansion of charters in the city.

Over the past 3 or 4 years, CMOs in particular have reorganized. As documented in this study, directors of marketing or communications are no longer stand-alone positions. With the goal of better integrating the various outreach, recruitment, and advocacy efforts, these directors now report directly to a chief external officer or vice president. All of the national CMOs in this study report having a vice president overseeing all of their external marketing and outreach. Titles such as a chief external officer or vice president of community outreach usually refer to these new positions. These leaders run teams that focus on marketing, community engagement, student recruitment, and advocacy. The director of marketing at a national CMO explained:

> [The Vice President of External Outreach] oversees five teams. One is Marketing and Communications. Another one is External Relations. External Relations is in charge of student recruitment, community engagement, and the charter. . . . They share with Team Legal and Compliance, but charter renewal. They would be helping the community rally around Charter Renewal. That team is year-round. The folks that are doing community outreach are the ones who are at the forefront of student recruitment.

In essence, today, these vice presidents oversee the concerted effort of the organization to promote their schools. In this configuration, the marketing and communications teams have become, as a few CMOs described, "consultants" to the recruitment and advocacy arms of the organizations, creating the materials—brochures, fliers, banners—that they will use in their outreach efforts. The investment of personnel and resources to edvertising is noteworthy. As the IRS 990 forms reveal, these VPs are now the top leaders and earners in their respective organizations (IRS, 2014a, b, c, d, e, g, h, i, j, k, l, m, n). Thus, their visions inform and influence the organization, potentially shifting the focus away from pedagogical innovations and toward innovations in edvertising.

Oversight and Compliance: Ensuring Brand Fidelity

All respondents shared that it is one thing to have a brand identity, or even a branding manual, and a completely different thing for a school to feel like it must comply with the central office's—be it district or CMO—vision of the brand. When discussing their experiences with compliance, the marketing directors' expectations varied, with some using terms such as *encouraging* or *directing*, and others mentioning *auditing*, and *dictating*. The general sentiment, however, was that getting schools to conform to branding expectations was, as a vice president of a local CMO shared, like "herding cats." The following quotation, from the director of marketing of a national CMO, exemplifies challenges regarding compliance:

> We had one school that was like, "Do we have to put [CMO name] on our uniforms, or can we just have kids wear plain polo shirts?" To which the answer is, "Yes, yes. Put [CMO name] on your uniforms. You can't just have a plain polo shirt." But we're finding now is that they're saying, "We want a purple sign." We're [marketing team] like, "Purple isn't in our color palette." They'll [principals] just randomly go to a vendor, not even tell us, and order a purple sign.

Administrators at the NYC DOE and local CMOs reported desiring brand fidelity, but expressed a degree of resignation about its general implementation. This was particularly true at the NYC DOE, where officials lamented about the decentralized nature of the department and their inability to control the implementation of their brand. As one director shared: "The schools are on their own. That's the other thing about that sort of thing, how fractured everything is. We kind of throw our hands up and say like that's the school's responsibility, they can have their own websites they can have their own Twitter feed." Similarly, but with a bit more teeth, the vice president at a local CMO shared: "We want our schools to work with us so that our designer can create a coherent look and feel across the board."

When probed about consequences for schools going "in their own direction," the vice president replied, "It's not ideal. We don't stop them if we find that they've done that. We don't make them tear down a poster that they created because it wasn't created by us. We just try to demonstrate for them that we have capacity in-house to handle those types of projects." This local CMO aspired for compliance, but allowed for school-level differentiation. The NYC DOE and smaller local CMO demonstrated more leniency in their approach to compliance, while the national CMOs took a stronger stance.

Concerned with aligning their brand across geographic regions and cultivating a national reputation, national CMOs had a more organized approach that involved audits. Describing her approach to compliance, the director of marketing at a national CMO shared: "I don't want to use the word *dictate*, that's too strong, but we just sort of dictate the colors issue, the signage issue, how big the sign should be, those types of things." Unlike the previous examples, this CMO expressed little tolerance for individuality. In fact, she further explained that there "are a lot of times, even if somebody [a principal] does something wrong, the regional heads will catch it and be like, 'It must come down,' or, 'No, you can't do it that way,' or, 'You have to communicate about this and this is the reason why.'"

When asked how organizations ensure fidelity, she shared: "Our CEO is on board, and therefore the executive team is on board, and then all of the regional leaders, get them on board because they get how important it is. So we've definitely done that, and so now when we have new leaders coming in, new teachers coming in, they don't know any different." This particular CMO ramped up its branding and marketing just over the past 5 years—later than many national organizations. As a result, they have been unifying and relaunching their brand while continuously expanding. The director of marketing, as the quote illustrates, had management's support in helping roll out the marketing efforts. She also shared that while some older principals were resistant to the changes—as it could mean changing school colors or their very logo—newly hired principals understood the expectations about branding and marketing, making fidelity to the brand less of an issue. This finding suggests that, when hiring, CMOs are actively searching for candidates who buy into and will effectively implement their marketing initiatives.

All CMOs reported having teams of individuals who visit schools to ensure compliance. Some encouraged alignment, while other actively measured it. At the larger, national CMOs, members of the regional leadership or operations teams visit schools. In explaining the purpose of these visits, the director of marketing at a national CMO shared that they are working directly with schools to help principals understand that "I can't do this because marketing and communications is the boss and they'll be mad at me, or I can't do this because it actually detracts from the overall brand."

One large, national CMO described having created a marketing assessment tool with various ratings for how well schools were implementing their brand. The director of marketing explained that their operations teams would go through the school and say, "I'm giving you a six out of seven" in terms of fidelity to branding principles. She further explained:

> We're [marketing team] working closely together with operations,
> so we just did an audit of all the schools in Connecticut, finding
> exemplars and nonexemplars as we call it. Ways people have
> diverged from the brand standards or upheld the brand standards.
> The Operations Team is going to use that in a presentation report to

director of school operations as a what to do, what not to do type of thing.

When probed about the results of the audit, she explained, "I would say most of them fall somewhere in the middle. There are pieces that are exemplar, and then there are pieces that are like, 'we wish you hadn't done that.' I think that's par for the course. I don't think most people at the school level necessarily care that their font is Rockwell. They want to educate kids."

These marketing audits are a key shift within education away from pedagogy and toward edvertising strategy. While principals may want to focus on educating their kids, as the director of marketing shared, they are being assessed on their compliance with, for example, using the Rockwell font. Here, edvertising has become yet another accountability measure with which principals must contend.

Aligning the Message: Reliance on Social Media

Nearly simultaneous to the expansion of the educational market in New York City, social media began to play a more prominent role in society at large. While the more competitive educational landscape is one factor in the changing marketing landscape, marketing as an industry independently was evolving toward an increased reliance on social media by parents and teachers alike. As the above-mentioned marketing teams reveal, this new focus pushed CMOs and the NYC DOE to build capacity by hiring personnel with experience in social media as well as website design and maintenance.

This allocation of staffing resources to social media personnel represents a proactive, rather than reactive, approach to control an organization's external message, and also an effort to protect an organization from inappropriate uses of social media that could damage their brand. The director of marketing at a national CMO voiced the sentiment of many of the participants when she shared that the digital media personnel were "able to streamline the communications, we're able to have a consistent and cohesive thread of communication." To this end, all participants reported daily monitoring of all social media platforms as well as set schedules to ensure that the content is current. A marketing director described her organization's social media outlets: "Facebook, Twitter, a blog, and Instagram, and that is managed by my team, primarily by my marketing communication associate." When prompted about updating the site, she shared that "at least one of those accounts is updated daily. We have three posts a week on Facebook. One post a week on the blog. Couple posts a week on Instagram and Twitter is every day, at least a retweet." Similarly, an official at the NYC DOE shared: "We have the digital specialist who's our social media person. I've a graphics specialist who is our designer and does all of our desktop layout."

This same official lamented the challenge of keeping websites current in a large and very politicized organization.

Particularly for geographically dispersed charter schools, social media provide an interesting and powerful way to streamline an institutional message. However, to coordinate schools around a branded identity requires central organization and a great deal of institutionally invested time and money. As these findings reveal, organizations have opted to make those investments in developing branded social media outlets with teams managing them.

Research shows that CMOs are ahead of other educational organizations in developing and consistently using social media as a branding and marketing tool (Jessen & DiMartino, 2016). While private schools also have the financial resources to push their message through this medium, Jessen and DiMartino find that CMOs are, surprisingly, much more sophisticated in using social channels to, for example, target a population beyond alumni for purposes of fundraising. Again, this speaks to greater institutional shifts in priorities, and the competitive needs of certain educational organizations.

Building Local Awareness: Community Outreach

Another critical piece in the evolution of marketing is community outreach. Referred to consistently across CMO interviews, community outreach represents a large part of their organizations' marketing efforts, which involves both concrete marketing materials as well as considerable personnel resources, specifically teams of people who go into communities to recruit students. Community outreach ranges from handing out fliers in front of daycares and churches to hosting community movie nights replete with free ice cream delivered from CMO-branded trucks. The vice president of a midsized CMO explained that community outreach was an integral part of the marketing of schools. In describing his organization's outreach, the vice president shared: "Sarah's [outreach leader] team will sometimes hire street outreach, so that would look different depending on the community. It may mean everything from just standing on a street corner near feeder schools and handing out fliers about the new charter school, or going into stores and leaving stacks of postcards." These efforts actively attempt to market to the neighborhood in which the charter is embedded, as well as to build brand awareness. Embedding personnel into communities is a particularly strategic initiative. As we saw in Chapter 1, word of mouth is one of the most impactful marketing tools, especially when it comes from a trusted neighbor or a local source. CMOs' focus on building community networks—via on-the-ground personnel and repeated community events—reflects their desire to grow grassroots support and energy for their particular brand.

In New York City, pro–charter school educational advocacy networks have also been instrumental in building capacity around community outreach. The goal of the organization, Families for Excellent Schools, Inc. (FES), is to "train and organize parents for sustained community action and to influence educational policy"(IRS, 2014f). FES works in tandem with CMOs in New York City to increase awareness and support of charter schools. In effect, FES builds the capacity of local actors to market charter schools to their neighbors, creating a powerful, pro-charter word-of-mouth network.

As these data illustrate, organizations' marketing efforts are becoming increasingly sophisticated, and have become fully integrated into their financial and governance structures. This is particularly true of CMOs in the New York City region, who have been driving the competitive landscape of educational marketing, as we will see in the next section. This dedication of considerable financial resources—both in materials and in personnel—speaks to CMOs' perceived need to differentiate themselves in a competitive marketplace. It also marks an organizational focus shift toward proactively engaging in marketing in order to "compete," rather than by making improvements in pedagogy or practice.

Checking Out the Competition: The Market Leaders

Perceptions of who was being competed against varied by the scope of an organization. The larger or national CMOs competed against one another for teachers and students. The smaller, local CMOs focused on recruiting locally for their niche school market. Finally, in contrast to them all, the NYC DOE representation shared that they felt little competitive pressure from the outside actors because they had a "captured audience."

National CMOs were very aware of the work of their charter peers. The director of marketing at a national CMO shared: "In New York, it's getting to be an increasingly crowded market. If you're a teacher and you want to teach in New York City, and you want to teach at a high-performing public charter school, I would imagine you're probably applying to Achievement First, KIPP, Uncommon [Schools], Success [Academies], maybe Democracy Prep. The world is your oyster!"

In markets where many larger CMOs are competing for teachers and students, brand awareness becomes key. Every CMO interviewed for this study highlighted KIPP and Success Academies as being the "market leaders" in the field: the organizations that dedicated the most financial resources to marketing and branding. As one director of marketing described, "Success Academy is the gold standard of having every one of their schools look exactly the same. We're never going to get quite there, and it's not our goal, nor do we have the budget to get there, but we think our schools can look a bit more uniform than they do."

While charter and district organizations identified Success Academies as the brand leader in New York City, they identified KIPP public charter schools as the national brand leader. One of the oldest and most established CMOs, KIPP is over 20 years old and operates in 20 states. KIPP's longstanding, carefully modeled reputation has brought it to a new place in terms of marketing and branding. Rather than spending on advertising campaigns, they now can work on crafting and maintaining their organization's story. An executive at a national marketing firm that works with CMOs described this shift:

> You see schools like KIPP, they're doing something a little bit different. Because they've got such a great brand and they've got such a great story to tell, you start to shift as a school when you get into these large, not only just number of schools but because your reputation is so good. . . . You've seen KIPP over the last few years transition largely away from paying for ads and getting out there to producing these beautiful stories about their students and their teachers and leveraging those stories in 30 pre-roll spots on YouTube or just simply doing great minute to 2-minute videos on YouTube and then activating them in their social networks in really creative ways.

The transition from "paying for ads" to recruit new students to "producing beautiful stories" about the organization illustrates how established KIPP has become within the educational marketplace. Given KIPP's national reach and influence, it could also be predictive of the future of educational marketing.

In contrast, the smaller, local CMOs shared that they do not see themselves competing with the large national CMOs, but rather with their own particular niche within the marketplace. The vice president of a local CMO described the situation this way: "We're in a somewhat different space from the KIPPs or the Success Academies, given that we're focused on the secondary level and there aren't too many other charter high school operators at that level." Here, being in a "niche" market gives them a more secure applicant pool, and potentially shields the organization from some of the intense charter school competition at the elementary and middle school level.

For a different reason, a director at the NYC DOE reported not feeling pressure from these market leaders in the charter market either. He explained the NYC DOE has "a captured audience. People have to come to us. We don't have to sell them on the schools." The NYC DOE official further clarified that their challenge is communication, such as in sending notification to parents regarding key public school programs and events, rather than competition from outside players. Here, marketing and branding is used to promote public service campaigns across the city rather than to compete for student headcount.

Isomorphism in the Marketplace

Another trend apparent from the example of New York City is that some of the partner support organizations that emerged with the small schools movement and then grew under the Bloomberg administration in New York City have since changed direction, becoming CMOs. This is best exemplified by New Visions for Public Schools and Urban Assembly, both originally school partners, which now formally manage charter schools in New York City. Similar to established CMOs, these new CMOs have begun embracing branding and marketing practices with zeal. Indeed, New Visions for Public Schools has developed its own branding manual for new school leaders.

There has also been a rise in for-profit, independent schools. Some of these schools, while independent and nonpublic in New York City, are part of larger, national charter school networks. This is best exemplified by Basis Independent Brooklyn, which is affiliated with the larger Basis Charter School Network. We think it no coincidence that Basis heavily emphasizes branding and marketing.

These findings reveal fluidity within the educational management landscape, with school managers transforming from public school partners to school managers to, in some cases, private schools. This raises important questions about the factors that push management organizations to evolve, and particularly the role of funding, both public—federal, state, and local— and foundational, in shaping the organizations' visions and, ultimately, their relationships with schools (DiMartino, 2014). The marketing and branding decisions of these organizations are particularly important to capture as they rebrand and promote themselves in the educational marketplace.

COMPENSATING THE NEW EXECUTIVES

Given that we have clearly seen an evolving organizational emphasis on marketing, the question naturally follows: How much financial investment is being expended in such efforts? This section, expanding on the previous one, examines the compensation, tenure, and experience of these new leaders within public education. Data from IRS 990 forms and SeeThroughNY, the New York State public employee database, provide useful information about compensation. It is important to note that the 990 forms are self-reported and provide information on the highest-compensated employees in the organizations. Table 2.1 gives an overview of the salaries of the organizational leaders involved in marketing and branding in the organization. Organizational websites and the social networking site LinkedIn were used to gather additional information regarding job descriptions and prior experience.

As Table 2.1 illustrates, in general, nationally oriented CMOs, those looking to expand beyond a single state, tend to have vice president or executive officer positions that encompass marketing, branding, communications, and community outreach. The average salary for this position was $180,000, ranging from $161,000 at Uncommon Schools to $201,162 at KIPP. A few of the local CMOs also had these executive positions, most notably Success Academy and New Visions for Public Schools. Success Academy, while local to New York City, operates a large number of schools—over 22—with aspirations to open more. Interestingly, New Visions for Public Schools was historically a support partner to district public schools in New York City. Recently, however, it began opening charter high schools across New York City.

The local management organizations that had these executive-level positions compensated their employees at rates similar to their national peers. In terms of professional experience and educational background, the majority of these leaders had prior experience in the private sector and possessed graduate degrees in business. Additionally, the data reveal that, almost without exception, individuals were hired into these positions within the past 4 or 5 years. This corresponds with the previous section, which reports on the ramping up of marketing and branding practices during this time period.

The smaller, local charter schools tended to have little capacity regarding marketing and branding. These organizations, such as the Explore Network and Public Prep, reported no vice president of external affairs or director of marketing on their IRS 990 forms. Their IRS 990 forms tended to have data on school-level positions, such as principals.

As a point of reference, the NYC DOE is included in this table. While it is a local player, the NYC DOE is also the largest school district in the nation. An evaluation of the NYC DOE's organizational chart (NYC DOE Organizational Chart, 2017) revealed that there is no clearly dedicated senior executive—at the deputy chancellor level—in charge of marketing, branding, and communications. As noted earlier, the NYC DOE did open a marketing department in 2012. The current director earns $117,470, which is notably less than his CMO counterparts. In terms of salaries, it is important to note that the chancellor of New York City's public schools earns $226,811, a sum that is not too different from the highest-paid national charter school executives. This shows both the amount of financial resources available to CMOs for branding and marketing, especially as compared to a school district, but also the value the CMOs place on these positions, potentially at the expense of more academic positions.

Table 2.1. Roles, Experience, and Compensation of Marketing and Communications Personnel

Organization	Title	Tenure	Previous Position	Education	Compensation	Position Descriptors
Ascend Learning Inc.	Managing Director of Communications and Development	1	nonprofit organization	PhD	n/a	Communications, Marketing, Development
Explore Network	No data					
Family Life Academy Network	No data					
Harlem Village Academies	External Affairs and Administrative Director	n/a	n/a	n/a	$117,470	External Affairs and Communications
Icahn Charter Schools	None					
New Visions for Public Schools	Vice President of External Affairs	4	public relations	MBA	$171,156	
New York City Department of Education	Director of Marketing and Digital Communications	4	government agency	MA	$117,320	Communications, Brand Awareness, Advertising, Digital and Social Media
Public Prep	No data					
ROADS Network	Chief Executive Officer	4	nonprofit organization	EdD	$154,232	External Relations, Communications

Organization	Title	Tenure	Previous Position	Education	Compensation	Position Descriptors
Success Academy Charter Schools, Inc.	Executive Vice President of Public Affairs and Communications; Managing Director of Marketing	4; 6	publishing; Fortune 500 company	MBA	$195,208 $157,500	Communications, Marketing, Public Affairs Communications, Brand Awareness, Advertising, Digitial and Social Media
Achievement First	Chief External Officer	4	nonprofit organization	MBA	$188,447	Marketing, Communications, Community Development, Advocacy
Democracy Prep	Director of Communications	n/a	n/a	n/a	$121,032	Communications
KIPP Public Charter Schools	Chief Strategy Officer	4	management consultant	MBA	$201,162	Communications, Marketing, Government Affairs, Advocacy
Uncommon Schools	Chief External Officer	5	Fortune 500 company	MBA	$161,438	Communications, Marketing, Advertising, Digital and Social Media

Note. Data for this table comes from multiple sources (IRS, 2014a, b, c, d, e, f, g, h, i, j, k, l, m, n)

MAKING SENSE OF THE NEW EXECUTIVE CLASS IN PUBLIC EDUCATION

In this chapter we have documented the emergence of a new class of managers that has emerged over the past 20 years. While the goals and foci of the new managers vary depending on their national versus local orientation and size, their existence marks an institutional shift within public education. The growth and centralization of edvertising activities is indicative of increasing institutional prioritization of competitive strategizing through external image nmanagement. Within the market-driven framework, organizations employ a variety of edvertising tactics to increase their market share. The explosion of social media, in particular, has enabled educational organizations, particularly large CMOs, to systematically align and distribute their message even when their individual schools are geographically dispersed. This has coerced even smaller charter chains and autonomous schools to enact, and invest in, similar practices in efforts to keep apace (DiMaggio & Powell, 1983).

Larger and nationally oriented CMOs are at a distinct advantage in this system because they have strategically built up their marketing and branding departments to support large-scale recruitment and outreach efforts. Systematic, organized, and effective, these concerted marketing efforts, especially in recruitment, directly affect their schools' enrollment, and in turn, the resources that the organization receives via per-pupil funding. These organizations' use of highly glossified branded materials—from direct mailers to brochures, social media outlets, and on-the-street outreach—allows them to craft campaigns to targeted communities.

In contrast, smaller and local CMOs do not have the organizational capacity or the financial resources to compete with the larger, national CMOs. In these smaller CMOs, marketing responsibilities are folded into other responsibilities—but are not unique, highly paid, stand-alone positions. As a result, these organizations do not have the glossy brochures or direct mailers sent to potential applicants' homes. In addition, they do not have the personnel to monitor social media sites or do on-the-street outreach.

This lack of organizational and financial capacity for marketing obviously places their brands at a disadvantage compared to their more strategically branded competition. This finding surfaces a tension within the charter school sector, specifically between larger or nationally oriented CMOs and smaller organizations. Akin to tensions between national fast-food chains, such as McDonald's, and smaller, more localized restaurants, it will be interesting to see how these two groups function within the same communities, especially as the marketplace becomes increasingly crowded.

Organizationally speaking, we see institutional isomorphism taking place as institutions invest similar amounts of money in executive salaries. Taking a values lens to the compensation data, we can infer that, in the aggregate, national CMOs in this data set value the role of marketing director slightly more highly than do the smaller CMOs or public districts. With more autonomy to allocate salaries, focused spending at the CMO level allows for an institutional emphasis on marketing. The disaggregated salary data indicate that the market leaders are able to tap into economies of scale, and the institutional memories of their consumers, while local chains strive to keep up (DiMaggio & Powell, 1983).

Within these highly marketized and increasingly privatized landscapes, as this chapter documents, a new set of actors—with specialized pedigrees and training—has emerged. These marketing executives and their affiliated organizations are part of a directed move to further commoditize public education. This shift is best illustrated in the language used by the new executives. Parents and students are "consumers" to be "targeted" with specific "messages" in the hopes of "driving" enrollment. Using Weick's (1995) sensemaking framework, this is the time for practitioners—from the private and public sector—to reflect on their new roles as marketing executives within the public sector: specifically, to examine how they are enacting corporate principles within the public sector, and to further make sense of how their actions might have larger consequences on the very essence of public education.

In this chapter we have chronicled the ascent of a new class of managers within public education. This shift raises numerous ethical concerns that require attention. Data from this chapter reveal that many of these new educational leaders come from outside education, bringing their business acumen to public education. As top management, their experiences will influence the direction of the organization at all levels. More personnel and financial resources, as exemplified by several CMOs, will be allocated to edvertising efforts. As money in education is finite, a choice to highly compensate marketing managers potentially redirects resources away from other, more academic areas. This raises ethical questions: Should public money be spent on ratcheting up marketing campaigns or on improving pedagogy, capital improvements, or something else?

We also see from our interviews with marketing directors new hiring criteria for principals and additional expectations placed upon them. Amenability to further an organization's edvertising efforts is a new attribute of an attractive applicant, as it will be this principal's responsibility to implement edvertising efforts at the school level—efforts, in the case of some CMOs, that will be audited by compliance officers. This added responsibility conveys clear organizational values to candidates, and has the potential to shift principals' time and energy away from instructional leadership.

Finally, in this chapter we learned about CMOs' embrace of community outreach efforts to boost enrollment. Street outreach, ice cream socials, movie nights, and other community-oriented efforts are lovely. But it is important to reflect on who is sponsoring these events—community outsiders, not insiders. These are not community events cultivated by local members;

rather, they are manufactured events with the overarching goal of driving charter school enrollment. While corporate sponsorship has long been a part of society, this direct attachment to public education is new. Here again, national CMOs with foundational and corporate support have many more resources to pull from to build and sustain these efforts, and it shows. In this respect, districts and their autonomous charter school counterparts are poor competitors on an increasingly uneven playing field.

This chapter has begun to examine these new actors within public education, but there is need for more research. Notably, national CMOs, with their established marketing arms, are poised to expand their market share within this pro-choice environment. The question arises: What will happen to the smaller, local charter management organizations and autonomous charter schools? How will districts—large and small—respond to these increasingly competitive environments? Will this competition lead to an even increased emphasis branding and marketing practices? If so, how will this affect school budgets—across types (district and charter)—in the years to follow? Given the current inequitable allocation of resources—financial and human—across public education, these are pressing areas for future investigation.

CHAPTER 3

"An Expression of Values"
Four Case Studies of Edvertising Budgets

"The budget is not just a collection of numbers, but an expression of our values and aspirations."

—Jacob Lew, Former Director
of the White House Office of Management and Budgets

"You can tell a lot about an organization's priorities by how they spend their money."

—Success Academy Charter Network Website, 2011

Money is not just money. The way we as individuals choose to spend our own money speaks to our values and priorities. The same is true for government entities, private companies, and nonprofit organizations, as reflected in the quotes above. As quasi-markets in education have expanded in cities throughout the country, budgets have shifted to fit the new priorities.

As we began to see in Chapter 2, one of the emerging priorities in response to market-like competition is edvertising. At a most basic level, the organizations involved in public education are beginning to invest in marketing. This leads to a broader question: How much money overall is being allocated to attract students and parents, teachers, and potential investors?

To date, as Chapter 1 revealed, examinations of budgetary expenditures on marketing and branding in traditional public and charter schools have been limited. This is partly because marketing in education is in its naissance, and some institutions have yet to think strategically about how to effectively create targeted campaigns. However, there is mounting evidence that many charter schools—particularly those managed by private and nonprofit organizations (educational management organizations known as EMOs and CMOs, respectively)—are increasingly invested in developing well-established brand identities and expansive marketing campaigns. These organizations are seemingly leading edvertising practices in a manner toward which other educational players in these quasi-markets are only

45

beginning to strive. Yet, because of their privately managed organizational structure, CMOs and EMOs are not always required to report their budgets to the same degree as public schools and districts. Transparency for these organizations is a persistent issue—perhaps most particularly regarding finances.

Increased spending on edvertising has serious implications for funding considerations. Given constricting educational budgets nationwide, developing and sustaining marketing and advertising campaigns could mean reallocating already scarce funds away from pressing institutional needs. However, marketing dollars compound. Strong brands and powerful marketing campaigns are retained in our collective memories—sometimes long term. For example, when we ask if you remember the commercial that sang, "I'd like to buy the world a _____," most of us will instantly fill in the word "Coke," reinforcing just how clearly some ads are retained in our memories. In short, a strong initial campaign does not need to be an annual expense. In fact, the stronger the marketing campaign or brand, the less money an organization has to subsequently spend.

For educational institutions, this means that unlike capital spent on operating costs, facilities or teacher salaries, advertising, marketing, or branding money does not necessarily "disappear" after the first year it is spent. This is particularly true for branding, which simply requires maintenance, once developed. Thus, if a school elects to invest a significant portion of its budget on marketing in 1 year, the message that gets out might continue to resonate with potential consumers and community members through individual memory and social networks.

To a degree, this makes an analysis of marketing and branding dollars more complex than simply compiling a data set. An organization can spend large sums of money on a marketing campaign, but if it does not resonate with the intended consumer, it will not have been successful. On the other hand, organizations with more well-established brands, such as KIPP, have become market leaders in the industry, and so might not need to invest as much money as they likely did at the outset in developing their brand identity.

Nevertheless, given our broad interpretation of budgets being indicative of institutional values, the fact that money is being allocated to edvertising is suggestive of its growing significance and prioritization. With this in mind, we return to our primary focus on the landscape of edvertising practices across key organizational fields by evaluating the budgetary allotments and financing behind edvertising. In an attempt to shed some light on these expenditures, this chapter presents case studies of budgetary spending on marketing, advertising, and branding in four different regions: New Orleans; Washington, DC; Massachusetts; and New York. Using publicly available budgets on a variety of schools in these regions, we examine edvertising costs.

FOUR CASE STUDIES

For each region, school-level budgets were collected from publicly available sources, and line items reflecting marketing, recruiting, and advertising spending were compiled.* As noted in the Appendix, the majority of these data are self-reported, relying, at least in part, on administrators' interpretations of what constitutes marketing. In addition, different regions exhibit varying degrees of consistency in using marketing terminology. Thus, using these budgets, we looked for trends in each region separately

New Orleans

To understand the New Orleans public school system, you must begin with Hurricane Katrina. In 2005, before Katrina made landfall, the school system in New Orleans was deeply troubled—plagued by intense poverty, systemic inequity, persistent segregation, and even institutional corruption (Hill & Hannaway, 2006). According to Hill and Hannaway (2006), New Orleans was one of the worst-performing school systems in the country. Once the hurricane had destroyed most of the city's infrastructure, including the public schools, neoliberal educational reformers quickly, and controversially, seized on the devastation as an "opportunity" to create an educational laboratory, built on Chubb and Moe's (1990) vision of a market-based system of schools.

Within a few months of the hurricane, Hill and Hannaway (2006) published a plan calling for engaging private-sector companies to fund the market-based reforms, and focusing on the integral involvement of large educational management organizations, such as KIPP, Edison, Teach for America, and New Leaders for New Schools, to "developing functioning schools quickly" (p. 6). They argued that officials should "appeal directly to Aspire, KIPP, and other national charter and contract school providers" (Hill & Hannaway, 2006, p. 6). This plan is essentially what came to pass. The Recovery School District (RSD), which existed in a smaller portion of the city before the hurricane, was given control of more than 100 New Orleans schools, and private organizations were contracted to build a system of charter schools and citywide choice. Teachers were recruited for many of these charters primarily though Teach for America, and New Leaders for New Schools established a contract for principals in the city. According to a report from the Cowen Institute's Babineau, Hand, and Rossmeier (2017), 93% of students are currently enrolled in a charter school. Most large charter networks (e.g., KIPP and ReNEW) operate within the Recovery School District, while the city's five traditional public schools are managed by the

---

*Since the data collection process was slightly different for each region, we describe our data collection in detail in the Appendix.

Figure 3.1. Orleans Parish School Board Enrollment by School Type, 2009–2016

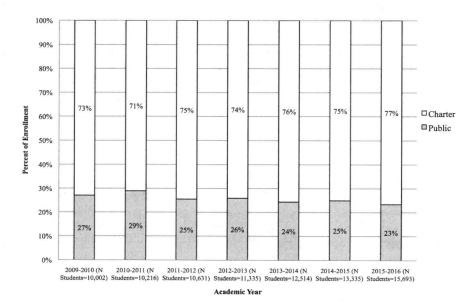

Orleans Parish School Board (OPSB), which also oversees several (mostly autonomous) charter schools. Babineau, Hand, and Rossmeier (2017) report that these five traditional public schools are intended to be converted to charter schools in the coming years. KIPP and ReNEW, which are discussed in detail in Chapter 6, are some of the largest CMOs in the city, by percentage of student enrollment and number of schools.

As noted in the Appendix, data for this case come from the Orleans Parish School Board from academic years 2009–2010 to 2016–2017. Figure 3.1 shows the enrollment trends in the OPSB over the years for all schools (both traditional public and charter) that fall under the OPSB governance. While the overall population of students being served by OPSB has increased over the past 6 years, Figure 3.1 shows that the charter schools under OPSB governance have gradually been occupying a larger portion of that overall student population. Whereas in 2009–2010, the public schools constituted roughly 30% of the OPSB enrollment, they are now closer to 20%. Yet while this trend is seemingly steady, it is not extremely rapid—particularly given the overall initiative in New Orleans to move toward an entirely charter system.

Compare the data of enrollment trend in Figure 3.1 with the "advertising" budgets of the charter and public schools in OPSB. Figure 3.2 shows the percentage of charter and public school budgets allocated to "advertising" during roughly the same time period shown in Figure 3.1. Although it

Figure 3.2. Orleans Parish School Board: "Advertising" Line Item as Percent of Overall Budget, 2009–2017

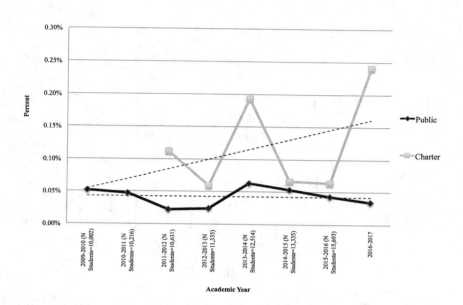

is clear that the proportion of the budget allocated to advertising is minimal (in aggregate, averaging less than .5%), trend lines in Figure 3.2 show that, on average, charter schools have increased their advertising budgets while public schools have essentially held steady. Overall, charter allocations toward advertising have swung dramatically year to year, yet still increased much more rapidly than the advertising allocations of the public schools. The rate of increasing budgetary allocations for advertising far outstrips the pace of enrollment in the charter schools, and runs in opposition to declining enrollments in OPSB public schools.

We also examined the advertising budget data by looking at per-pupil spending. One primary purpose of spending money on marketing is to attract and enroll students. A good way to comparatively measure advertising spending would be to look at the number of student applicants to an individual school, which is indicative of the return on investment of the marketing. Given that we did not have access to application data for the OPSB schools, we used student enrollment data as a proxy. In theory, one can view these data as the amount spent to enroll each student. Figure 3.3 shows per-pupil spending for charter and public schools in OPSB.

In most academic years, Figure 3.3 illustrates that charter schools in the OPSB are outspending their traditional school counterparts per pupil. The price of advertising per pupil in charter schools hits its peak at $16.36 in

Figure 3.3. Orleans Parish School Board: "Advertising" Line Item, Per Pupil, 2009–2016

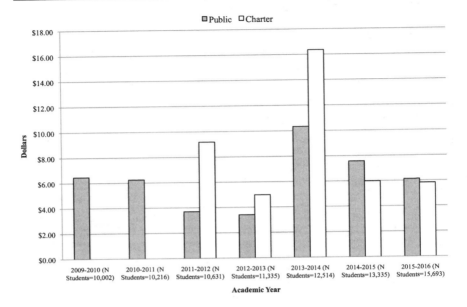

2013–2014. Interestingly, the charter schools and public schools follow a parallel trend, with a sharp increase in 2013–2014, followed by a decline to present. Given the autonomous budgeting of charter schools, this similarity potentially suggests the role of outside forces or locally compounding political pressures leading to a sweeping focus on edvertising efforts. It is worth noting that this is roughly the time period in which edvertising activities were taking off in New York City (see Chapter 2).

As mentioned earlier, because the OPSB represents only a subset of the schools in the district, and many of the CMO-led charters are housed in the RSD, these data cannot provide a complete picture of the edvertising that occurs through the city of New Orleans. They do highlight some important trends that are worth reviewing, given the extent of market-like structures in the city of New Orleans, combined with the autonomous budgeting of the charter schools. There appears to be a relationship between marketing expenditures and school type. We see a pattern of charter schools outspending traditional public schools on marketing, and a relative increase in spending on these activities over time. To some degree, this can be expected, given that some of these schools are likely newly created. Overall, however, these advertising budgets represent a very small portion of the OPSB school budgets—not yet reaching 1% on average of the average annual budget.

Most of these data do not reflect the marketing and brand awareness associated with CMOs, however. Critically, none of the charter schools included in this data set is managed by the larger or national charter management networks, which predominantly operate institutions in the Recovery School District. Also, as we will see in Chapter 6, sometimes schools in New Orleans employ low-cost marketing strategies involving employing teachers as free labor recruiters and social media managers.

Finally, the data reflected in the above figures do not account for the strategic marketing prowess and financial buttressing of recruiting teaching staff done by Teach for America or TeachNOLA in New Orleans. Advertising and marketing for the purpose of teacher recruitment was a finding in Chapter 2, and as we will see in Chapter 6, integral in New Orleans. The budget for teacher recruiting is particularly of note when considering the "advertising" budget for the traditional public schools in OPSB. In each of their annual budgets, OPSB disaggregated the offices accounting for each portion of this line item. Figure 3.4 shows OPSB's annual allocation of the advertising budget, which was managed either by the finance or human resources (HR) offices.

According to these data, human resources steadily increased its spending on advertising up through the 2015–2016 year. Given the organizational function of HR, one can assume that this was likely with the intent of recruiting teachers or staff. The charter schools in the OPSB do not similarly disaggregate their "advertising" budget. With this in mind, one should reconsider the above analyses as well, given that a portion of the advertising budget might be assumed to be going toward recruiting teachers—not just students.

Yet at its largest ($7,500 total for the 2015–2016 academic year), this OPSB's HR budget for recruiting at traditional public schools pales in comparison to the estimated teacher recruiting budgets for Teach for America in New Orleans. Currently, Teach for America is reportedly seeking a $5 million appropriation from the Department of Education in order to recruit approximately 400 new teachers for the New Orleans region. That would amount to roughly $12,500 per recruited teacher (Louisiana State Legislature, 2016). The majority of these funds will likely go to marketing efforts for Teach for America to advertise to potential candidates. We will discuss more of the relationship between Teach for America and New Orleans schools in Chapters 6 and 8.

The data from Orleans Parish School Board are significant because we begin to see a trend of the institutionalized differences in the approach to engagement in the market, as represented by variations in spending on advertising. All of these schools are working under the same immediate organizational governance—Orleans Parish School Board—in the same city, which, we can infer, imbeds them within similar political structures. As a city with universal choice and a common application (OneApp), they are each engaging in a similar market-like system. Perhaps even more interestingly, none of these charters is managed by a management organization,

Figure 3.4. Orleans Parish School Board Traditional Public Schools "Advertising" Line Item, Designated Office (HR or Finance), 2009-2017

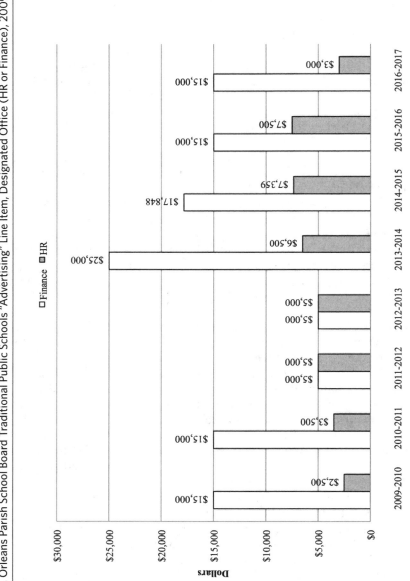

which might give them access not only to more extensive marketing resources, but might also allow them to attach themselves to a pre-established school brand. Thus, these schools are operating within a similar educational ecosystem.

One thing that is critically different between the public schools and their charter counterparts is the degree of control they have on their individual budgets, as evidenced by their disaggregated and inconsistent reporting structures. Potentially more fundamentally, they are influenced by the philosophical space that their school type occupies. Longitudinal data on advertising show, in general, that the charter schools are slightly outspending the public schools run by the OPSB. We cautiously infer from this trend that the charter schools in OPSB are organizationally prioritizing advertising more than the public schools. Given that both the public schools and the charter schools are operating within the same market-like ecosystem in New Orleans, this budgetary trend is further indicative of an educational values shift.

Washington, DC

The reputation of the public education system in Washington, DC, has been among the worst in the country. This has led to the promotion and development of a variety of school choice policies, including charter schools and a politically contentious federally funded voucher program.

The DC Public Charter School Board is the governing body for charter schools in the Washington, DC, area. They provide a great deal of detail on the local area charter schools, including annual budgets. Although all charter school budgets are submitted to the DC Public Charter School Board, they are not in a standardized form. Figure 3.5 shows the school-by-school comparison of the charter schools that have an itemized marketing budget. As noted in the Appendix, KIPP DC includes 16 individual schools, and both the Eagle Academy PCS and the Hope Community Charter Schools network each operate two schools in Washington, DC, the list of charters included in this data set represent thirty (31) of the approximately 118 charter schools which are currently operating in Washington, DC, or 26.2% of the charter market in the city.

As Figure 3.5 illustrates, there was a wide range of budgetary investment in marketing in 2015–2016. Like the data from New Orleans, these data show that very few schools are spending more than 1% of their expenditures on advertising. When examining these data, however, it is critical to think about the ways in which marketing works. Private companies that engage in marketing for similar products compete for what is known as "share of voice" (Jones, 1990). Share of voice is defined as a brand's portion of the total spending for a product category. In other words, companies are competing to get the attention of consumers, and the amount invested in a marketing campaign by one company is equivalent to the share of notice

Figure 3.5. Washington, DC Charter Schools Percent Spent of Total Expenditures on Marketing and Recruiting

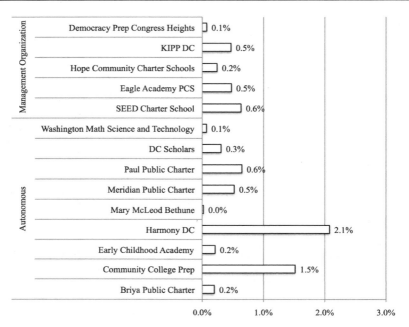

they will get from potential customers. In the world of educational marketing, the concept of share of voice is very relevant, as while not all parents and students are looking for the same *type* of educational experience, all students are required to look for some type of school.

We analyzed the Washington, DC, charter school marketing data for share of voice—that is, functionally speaking, if you are a parent in the city, which charter school's "voice" you would hear the loudest. Figure 3.6 shows the breakdown of these data, which simply designates a proportion to each school based on its total spending on marketing in 2015–2016. Given that these data comprise only 29% of the charter landscape in the city, they cannot provide a complete picture of the edvertising activities, or all of the "voices." In addition, we must recall that some edvertising activities are more costly than others, but not necessarily more impactful, which has the potential to skew 1 year of data. However, Figure 3.6 provides an interesting model to consider.

Based on this examination, KIPP DC charter schools have the dominant share of voice in this data set. Constituting 48.2% of the overall marketing capital spent among these charter schools, their portion is nearly equivalent to most of the other charter schools combined. Falling behind them in this analysis are Eagle Academy PCS (8.8%) and SEED charter school (8.7%)—both part of local management networks. In fact, Eagle Academy opened a

Figure 3.6. "Share of Voice" for Represented Washington, DC Charter Schools Marketing Budgets, 2015–2016

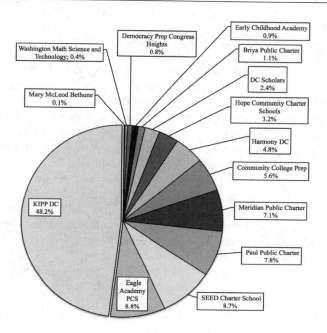

second campus in the 2015–2016 academic year—which might account for their marketing expenditures in this year.

Spotlight on KIPP DC. Because of the impact of KIPP in Washington, DC, as well as the national power of KIPP as a whole, we more closely examined the budgets for these schools.

For this analysis, because of the organization's consistency of reporting, we were able to collect and compare multiple years of budget data (from 2012 to 2016). As noted in the Appendix, Washington, DC, KIPP schools have three line items in their publicly available budgets that are indicative of marketing allocations: student recruitment, staff recruitment, and outreach. In order to gain clarity on the provision of "outreach," we directly contacted the KIPP DC offices. The vice president of operations and finance in KIPP DC indicated that outreach was frequently used for community-focused events that intended to, as he said, "build community awareness of KIPP" in the local area. He gave an example of a KIPP-sponsored community barbeque that had been recently hosted using this budget. At such events, KIPP has a visible presence, and is able to distribute branded and marketing materials—from fliers to t-shirts—to families in the area. The allocations also potentially support the two community outreach staff members recently added to the KIPP DC office (Venture Philanthropy Partners, 2015).

As discussed in Chapter 2, outreach events can be viewed as a means of integrating schools with local community, or, more critically, as opportunities to increase KIPP's brand awareness, and subsequently, the student applicant pool. The latter assumption aligns with some of KIPP DC's public documents about its reasons for community engagement. According to a report written by Venture Philanthropy Partners (2015), one major reason for community engagement was to enable KIPP to expand: "In order to grow aggressively, KIPP DC needed to establish deeper relationships with their local communities, including students and their families" (p. 3). Finally, as will be seen in Chapter 6, our interviews with teachers in New Orleans indicated that KIPP's outreach events in that city were organizationally viewed as recruiting opportunities. Given these factors, we included the outreach data in our marketing budget analysis for KIPP DC.

For the past 5 years, KIPP DC has spent an average of $469,850.20, annually, on student and staff recruiting and outreach. Figure 3.7 shows the yearly breakdown of this spending and highlights that a significant portion of KIPP DC's overall marketing budget is going toward the aforementioned "outreach" events. In no year does KIPP DC spend less than $200,000 on outreach, according to these data, and in 2 of the 5 years, spending crested over $300,000. Given the relative stability and magnitude of this investment, we can assume from these data that outreach is a marketing priority for KIPP DC.

Student and teacher recruitment represents another significant chunk of the advertising budget shown in Figure 3.7. The isolated line item "student recruitment," according to these budgets, represents the smallest portion of expenditures. It is still a significant amount, however, averaging $64,827.20 per year. With the existence of the category of "outreach" covering KIPP-sponsored local events, it seems reasonable that this allocation is less substantial. Staff recruitment averages $131,093.80 for KIPP DC. As KIPP DC opened several schools throughout the 5 years represented in Figure 3.7, it seems reasonable that the organization invested in teacher recruitment to fill new openings.

In examining these data, it is again important to return to a broader consideration about the nature of marketing, and with it, the educational ecosystem in which KIPP DC schools exist. The KIPP DC schools are all located on six "campuses" in Washington, DC. According to the KIPP website (2017), two of the campuses have opened since FY2012. Most of these campuses have multiple schools, usually representing successive grade levels. Thus, in theory, one student is able to enter into a campus for elementary school and stay through the middle school located in the same building. Questions can be raised as to whether the campuses are truly separate schools—particularly with respect to marketing practices.

We thus broke down KIPP DC's annual marketing budgets not only by school, but also by campus, as shown in Figure 3.8. According to this

Figure 3.7. KIPP DC Charter Schools Annual Budget Allocations for Staff Recruiting, Student Recruiting, and Outreach

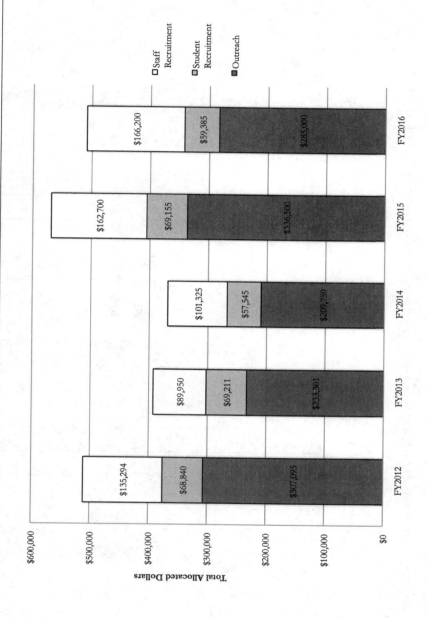

Figure 3.8. KIPP DC Charter Schools Total Annual Budget Allocations for Recruiting and Outreach: Average Amount Per School and Per Campus

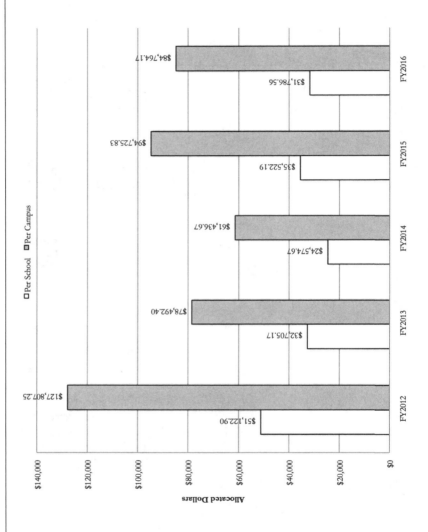

analysis, annually, KIPP DC spent between $61,437 and $127,807 per campus on recruiting and outreach activities. Figure 3.8 shows us that KIPP DC spent the most on marketing in FY2012, which is the same year in which it expanded from four to five campuses—allocating over $120,000 in marketing per campus, and over $50,000 per school. Marketing spending peaked again in FY2015.

Geography plays into our interpretation of these data. Two of the KIPP DC campuses are located in the southeastern/Capitol Heights region of Washington, DC in fairly close proximity, and still two others in the northeastern region the city. The most recently opened campuses are located close to older sites. Presumably, from an organizational standpoint, this allows the schools to expand to meet student demand. However, some of that demand can be manufactured through marketing. From a marketing standpoint, proximity of campuses allows newer schools to draw on neighborhood reputations and demand—some of which is attributed simply to brand awareness. Thus, a marketing campaign to open new campuses, which were already in close proximity to the older schools, would seemingly require less investment.

Spotlight on Democracy Prep Congress Heights and the Democracy Builders Fee. In examining further the Democracy Prep Congress Heights budget, one line item was noteworthy. It read, "Democracy Builders—Fee: $108,805." A note beside this line item in the budget indicated it was a "scholar recruiting organization fee." Democracy Builders is the nonprofit organization that originally founded the Democracy Prep charter schools. Although Democracy Prep has become the management organization in charge of the charter schools themselves, Democracy Builders remains the parent organization—one that now focuses on lobbying for choice policies.

According to an annual report from another Democracy Prep school—Democracy Prep Endurance Charter School (New York City)—Democracy Prep charter schools can enter into contract with Democracy Builders to manage their marketing and recruiting. Here, Democracy Prep Endurance describes the nature of this contract:

> The School entered into a consulting agreement with DBI [Democracy Builders, Inc.] to perform student recruitment and enrollment, family engagement, parent advocacy initiatives and training, and government relations. As compensation to DBI for these services rendered, the School shall pay to DBI an annual fee equal to 1% of the School's total per-pupil funding. (Democracy Prep Endurance, 2014)

Given the provision in the Democracy Prep Congress Heights budget, it seems plausible that their school has entered into a similar contract with Democracy Builders. Although this relationship is not explicit in their materials beyond this budget line, this relationship is seemingly indicative of a school within a management network having access to resources to assist with recruiting and marketing.

It is important to note that the Democracy Builders fee listed in the Democracy Prep Congress Heights budget was in addition to $46,215 allocated to "recruiting & marketing," $20,650 separately apportioned to "staff recruitment," and an item listed as "student recruitment supplement" for $55,000—all of which were taken directly from the school's budget. In total, this would amount to $230,670 in marketing and recruiting spending for 1 year at Democracy Prep Congress Heights, which constitutes 2% of their expenditures for that year, and $355.97 of marketing per enrolled student. That would be a heavier investment in recruiting activities.

But, more critically, the Democracy Builders fee allocation is an example of larger issues when interpreting and evaluating marketing and branding budgets. First, charter schools affiliated with a larger management organization have the advantage of accessing not only the existing power of the brand, but also the business networks imbedded within the organizations. As many of the primary CMOs attract marketing executives who have experience creating private-sector campaigns, as reviewed in Chapter 2, they bring resources to the table that public schools and autonomous charter schools may not have. In market-like structures, those with the knowledge of how to work the market are at an advantage.

In addition, we need to assume that privately managed charter schools are primarily imbedded with the organizational fields (Arum, 2000) of their management company—not necessarily within the district within which they are located. This is due, in part, to the fact that a school's continued use of the organizational brand is often contingent on having an ongoing relationship with the management company. Research has shown that a school cannot continue to use a management company's brand if the school secedes from the larger organization (DiMartino, 2009). Thus, it is in the interest of both the management company and the schools to have the affiliated schools pay fees for services to the organization, which at the very least, by default, would open the possibility of aligning themselves with the power of the preexisting marketing and branding of the organization.

In the case described above, the organization contracted marketing fees. Yet, as a whole, such relationships and payments are simply very hard to track, given the nature of the relationships between the charter schools and the organizations, and the relative lack of transparency or consistency across charter school budgets. In other words, we should assume that, although Democracy Prep has listed a marketing contract with its management organization, many other charter schools might have similar arrangements that are less marked, or perhaps not reported at all.

Massachusetts

According to the Massachusetts Department of Elementary and Secondary Education (2017), 39,670 pupils throughout the state were enrolled in 82 charter schools. The majority of charter schools in the state are located in and around the Boston metro area, with others in Worcester and Springfield. As the Appendix notes, this data set included all charter schools in the state.

In Massachusetts, autonomous charter schools as well as charter schools are operated by management companies, both nationally and locally based. Figure 3.9 categorizes the charter school recruiting/advertising data into three organizational structures types—autonomous schools, those managed by local CMOs, and those operated by national management chains.

According to our analysis, several of the local CMOs have pushed recruiting and advertising over the past several years. Local CMOs such as Excel, Pioneer, and UP Education have outspent many of the other CMOs—with the slight exception of Uncommon Schools, which is a national network. According to these data, autonomously run charter schools have allocated little, on average, to advertising over the past 2 years.

The expenses of these less-well-established CMOs—including that of Uncommon Schools—echo the pattern of spending to establish brand awareness. When a new brand enters a market, or when a brand is trying to expand its consumer base, the company commonly allocates more funds toward marketing in an effort to reach consumers. Many of these smaller CMOs are likely in the process of building broader brand awareness, so they must invest in marketing. In addition, networks with a smaller parent organization are more likely to have operational expenses, such as marketing, show up on their individual school budgets. Larger organizations may manage much of the marketing at the foundation level, which reduces individual school costs and the probability of these expenses showing up on school-level budget reports.

Because the data set includes charter schools from around the state, the Massachusetts Department of Education categorizes charter schools into four neighborhood types: Boston, urban,[†] suburb, and rural. Charter schools in each of these settings face different political, organizational, and competitive structures. We thus broke out the average spending on recruiting/advertising by region. Results show that the budget line item of recruiting/advertising varies dramatically among these four neighborhood types, as seen in Table 3.1.

In Table 3.1 we see that charter schools located within the boundaries of the Boston School District spend more than twice as much on recruiting/advertising on average than the next highest neighborhood category: urban

---

† This category includes urban-located schools that are not in Boston, but are scattered primarily throughout the Boston metro area.

Figure 3.9. Massachusetts Charter Schools Average Annual Percentage of Expenditures Spent on Recruiting/Advertising

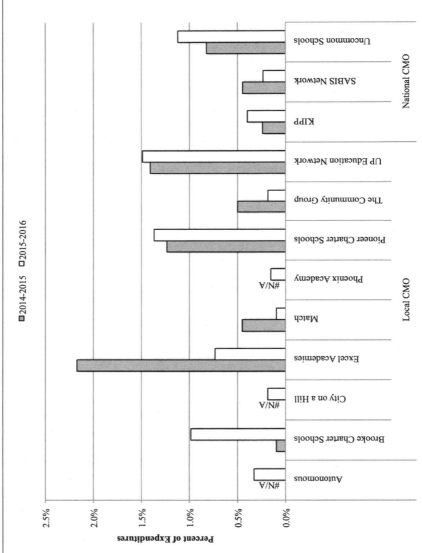

Table 3.1. Massachusetts Charter Schools, Average Amount Spent on Recruiting/Advertising in 2015, by Neighborhood Type

Neighborhood Type	Average Amount
Boston	$42,085.14
Urban	$20,440.51
Suburb	$12,254.86
Rural	$8,263.04

Table 3.2. Massachusetts Charter Schools, Average Spending on Recruiting/Advertising in 2015, By Region and Management Type

	Non-CMO	CMO
Boston	$18,171.96	$72,520.08
Suburb	$11,116.13	$19,087.22
Urban	$16,479.20	$30,739.93

charter schools. Subsequently, charter schools located in urban areas are spending nearly twice as much as suburban charter schools on advertising. Rural charter schools (although there are very few of them) are spending the least amount, on average.

From these data alone we can infer that schools in more highly competitive areas—those educational ecosystems with a greater density of institutional options and more market-like policy structures—are spending more on edvertising. Areas like Boston also have instituted policies of citywide choice, which allows students to enter into a market-like system, creating a necessary requirement on the supply—as well as the demand—side.

There are other logistical reasons for spending more on edvertising in urban areas. Charter schools located in areas with significant numbers of students who have access to public transportation have a wider geography of choice from which to potentially draw applicants. In summary, the greater the competition for students, the more fluid the choice policies, and the better access to a wider geography of students, the seemingly greater need to invest in recruiting and advertising.

We further disaggregated the data to explore the relationship that management structures might have with advertising expenditures. Table 3.2 shows the three regions of the state that have both autonomous charters and charters operated by management companies, and their relative spending on advertising.

The difference in recruiting/advertising spending in Boston, in particular, is dramatic. While CMO-operated charter schools in this region spend, on average, more than $72,000 on recruiting and advertising, autonomously managed charter schools spend only one-quarter of that amount. Although not as dramatic as the difference in Boston, the gap in budgetary allocations for autonomous and CMO-led charters persists in suburban and urban areas of the state. In urban areas outside of Boston, autonomously managed charter schools spend roughly half of what CMO-led charters spend on advertising and recruiting.

Echoing the patterns reviewed earlier, responding to competition, potential student demand, geographical freedom of public transportation, and in-place choice policies, we see again that charter schools in Boston and other urban areas have increased their emphasis on edvertising to a greater degree than suburban areas. Even autonomously led charter schools in the Boston area are spending more on edvertising than those in other urban areas or the suburbs—possibly indicating more intense competition for students.

A critical trend emerges in these data. In Massachusetts, we see the pattern of CMO-led charter schools outstripping the edvertising investments of autonomous charter schools. Given our ability to disaggregate by geographical region and management type with these data, our findings in Massachusetts speak not to marketing pressures from the political or geographical contexts in which the school are imbedded, but rather to a potential divergence in organizational values and cultures between CMO-led and autonomous charter schools.

This analysis does not take this finding a step further to compare public school spending on advertising with charter schools. While it is possible that public schools are spending roughly the same amount as charters on edvertising, one can infer from the lack of documentation on the detailed budgets that Massachusetts supplies that edvertising is likely not a financial priority. Yet even if Boston Public School's spending were equivalent to the local-area charters in raw dollars, proportional analysis is an important way to interpret the use of money. Within every budget, funds are limited. A choice to allocate a portion of those funds to one activity or cost inherently narrows the pool for other needs. Thus, given the broad transparency of Massachusetts and Boston public schools with respect to data, the lack of representation of edvertising spending on the Massachusetts school budgets signals a lack of institutional focus.

New York

As of 2018, 349 charter schools were approved to operate in New York State (New York State Department of Education, 2018). The Board of Regents and the State University of New York (SUNY) authorize the majority of charter schools in the state, with the New York City Department of Education authorizing a smaller share of schools. Some authorizers will tend to supervise certain networks of charter schools. SUNY, for example, is the authorizer of Success Academy Charter Schools and Achievement First Public Schools. In comparison, the Board of Regents is the authorizer for KIPP Academy Charter Schools, Democracy Prep, and New Visions for Public Schools.

Schools authorized by SUNY, in particular, provide useful information about the practices of edvertising. For this analysis, we examined budgets from SUNY-authorized charter schools' Annual Renewal Reports (ARR) from the 2012–2013 year (SUNY Charter Schools Initiative, 2017). Most of the 2012–2013 versions of SUNY's renewal reports include an itemized budget for all reviewed schools. In total, we were able to access budgets for 54 SUNY-authorized charter schools in New York.[‡] Each of these schools included a line item about marketing/recruiting/advertising—usually for both teacher and student recruitment. The data represented in this sample include five schools located outside of NYC—one each in Buffalo, Rochester, and Ithaca, and two in Albany—the majority of which, with the exception of the school in Buffalo, are autonomously managed.

Some of these budgets reported marketing and recruiting data split into two target consumers (staff and students), and some, notably Success Academies (as we will see later), included a third general category of "marketing/recruiting." In reviewing the 2012–2013 budgets for SUNY-authorized charter schools, some inconsistencies were evident—not in just the budget form, but also in recording the money allocated to each category. As we mentioned earlier, all of these data are self-reported. We suspect that these inconsistencies in reporting represents simply an inconstant and/or unclear definition of what constitutes marketing on the part of school leaders, reiterating the need for consistent and clear budget reporting in these areas.

Figure 3.10 shows the representation of schools by organizational manager in this analysis. These data show that while autonomously managed charter schools occupy both the largest portions of schools and students, Success Academy constitutes 24% of the schools represented, with Icahn Charter Schools and the ROADS network following.

Since there were many significantly represented management networks in these budgets, we disaggregated these data by operator first (Figure 3.11). The most notable finding here is that the budgetary allocations from Success Academy were so substantial, it is hard to visually represent them in comparison to all the other organizational networks authorized by SUNY. In 2012–2013, Success Academy spent about $3.5 million on marketing and recruiting in their New York City schools. The majority of this was spent on student recruiting, as shown in Figure 3.11. The next organization behind them is not really an organization at all; rather, it is a summative collection of the autonomous charter schools authorized by SUNY, which, in total,

---

‡ See the Appendix for details about data collection and analysis.

Figure 3.10. SUNY-Authorized Charter Schools: Percentage of Schools in Data Set by Organizational Management

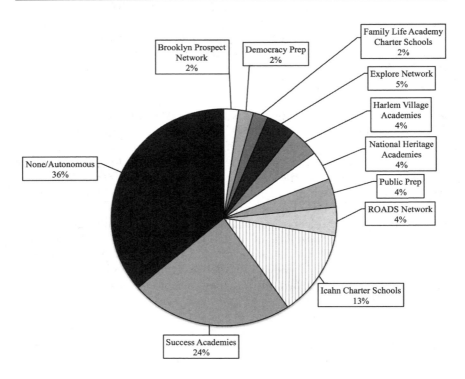

spent roughly $500,000 on marketing/recruiting activities in the same year. Note that autonomous charters constitute the greatest proportion of schools (36%) in this data set, however, so it would be expected that their total spending would be substantial.

Since Success Academy and the autonomous charters together constitute more than half of the schools in this data set, we sought to more effectively compare different organizations. We examined the average marketing spent by each network in Table 3.3, which illustrates the average amount that each organization spent on marketing and recruiting per school. On average, Icahn charter schools spent less than $2,500 while, at the other end of the spectrum, Success Academy spent over $320,000 on average per school in 1 year. Autonomous schools fall in the middle of this spectrum.

Clearly, a great deal of spending variability exists among the organizations. Networks such as Public Prep and Brooklyn Prospect Network

Figure 3.11. SUNY-Authorized Charter Schools, Total Amount Spent on Staff and Student Recruiting and Marketing, and "Other Recruiting and Marketing" in 2012-2013

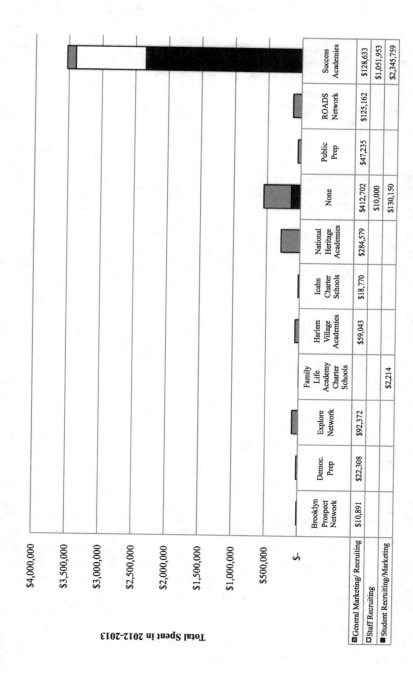

	Brooklyn Prospect Network	Democ. Prep	Explore Network	Family Life Academy Charter Schools	Harlem Village Academies	Icahn Charter Schools	National Heritage Academies	None	Public Prep	ROADS Network	Success Academies
General Marketing/ Recruiting	$10,891	$22,308	$92,372		$59,043	$18,770	$284,579	$412,702	$47,235	$125,162	$128,633
Staff Recruiting								$10,000			$1,051,953
Student Recruiting/Marketing				$2,214				$130,150			$2,345,759

Total Spent in 2012-2013

67

Table 3.3. SUNY-Authorized Charter Schools, Average Amount Spent on Marketing/
Advertising in 2012–2013 by Management

Management Network	Average Amount
Family Life Academy Charter Schools	$2,214.00
Icahn Charter Schools	$3,128.33
Brooklyn Prospect Network	$10,891.00
Democracy Prep	$22,308.00
Public Prep	$23,617.50
Harlem Village Academies	$29,521.50
None/Autonomous	$32,520.71
Explore Network	$46,186.00
ROADS Network	$62,581.00
National Heritage Academies	$142,289.50
Success Academies	$320,576.82

Table 3.4. SUNY-Authorized Charter Schools: Average Percentage of Total Expenditures Spent on Marketing/Recruiting in 2012–2013

Management Network	Average Percent
Family Life Academy Charter Schools	0.1
Icahn Charter Schools	0.1
Brooklyn Prospect Network	0.1
Democracy Prep	0.3
Harlem Village Academies	0.3
Public Prep	0.4
None/Autonomous	0.7
Explore Network	1.1
National Heritage Academies	1.5
ROADS Network	2.0
Success Academies	5.9

seemingly invested more heavily in staff recruitment, while Icahn and Family Life Academy Charter Schools spent money on student marketing/recruiting. Autonomous charters' spending on marketing and recruiting overall was fairly evenly spread among various advertising activitites. Some of the organizations that invested most heavily in student recruiting were national management organizations, including Uncommon Schools.

Many of these organizational networks have differently scaled resources and expenditure totals. Thus, we also looked at these data as percentages of each organization's overall expenditures (Table 3.4). As a percentage of the overall budgets of each of the networks, similar patterns to average

Table 3.5. Success Academy, Williamsburg and Cobble Hill: Functional Expenses Analysis of Per-Pupil Spending on Student Recruiting

School Name	Money Per Pupil
Success Academy, Cobble Hill	$2,561.72
Success Academy, Williamsburg	$2,904.10

spending emerge. At the bottom end of the spectrum is Family Life Academy Charter Schools and Icahn Charter Schools, while Success Academy tops the list.

Spotlight on Success Academy's Cobble Hill and Williamsburg Campuses. These findings led us to further inspect Success Academy's budgets, as they stood out not just among the SUNY-authorized charter school data, but also among most networks and schools in nearly every region we examined for this analysis.

Within the exceptional amounts of money spent on marketing by this network as a whole, two branch locations stood out: Cobble Hill and Williamsburg. Both of these schools were newly opened during this time period, having been authorized in September 2011, and enrolling their first students in the fall of 2012. The reports for these two schools note that expenses listed in the budgets are "for the period from September 13, 2011 (induction) to June 30, 2013." Given that this represents nearly two years of expenditures, we examined these campuses from a per-enrolled-pupil perspective. In effect, since there is only one student enrollment year on each of these campuses, we can interpret these data as the amount spent by the organization to fill each student seat.

Assuming that the parent organization (Success Academy), and not the school, is in charge of distributing funds and that their marketing team is driving the campaigns across the city, Success Academy allocated a significant amount of money on marketing at these particular schools. Table 3.5 highlights the numbers for Success Academy Williamsburg and Cobble Hill.

Both locations—Cobble Hill and Williamsburg—are located in Brooklyn in relatively wealthy and gentrified neighborhoods. As noted above, at this time, they were new schools, and so establishing themselves—and their share of voice—was likely viewed as organizationally critical. Success Academy Bedford-Stuyvesant II was also relatively new in this time period, but although they spent the third greatest amount per pupil on marketing for this school, the organization allocated only $1,009.53 per pupil for edvertising.

Yet, despite the potential other costs associated with starting new schools, student recruiting, according to their expense report, was one of

Table 3.6. Success Academy Williamsburg, Top Five Expenditures, 2011–2013

Budget Item	Expenditure
Salaries	$1,189,598.00
Student Recruitment	$291,187.00
Management Fee	$271,012.00
Payroll Taxes and Employee Benefits	$258,821.00
Instructional Supplies and Textbooks	$241,301.00
Teacher Recruitment	$49,767
Marketing	$56,908

Table 3.7. Success Academy, Cobble Hill: Top Five Expenditures from 2011–2013

Budget Item	Expenditure
Salaries	$1,341,365.00
Management Fee	$299,985.00
Student Recruitment	$266,667.00
Payroll taxes and employee benefits	$268,377.00
Instructional Supplies and Textbooks	$252,476.00

the highest spending categories in this time period for both schools. Table 3.6 shows the top five expenditure categories on Success Academy's Williamsburg budget. While one can expect salaries to constitute the top space in any educational budget, it is notable to have a recruiting/marketing item in the top five of spending categories. This student recruitment allocation does not include total amount spent on marketing and recruiting at Success Academy Williamsburg, however. Teacher recruiting totaled $49,767 at Success Academy Williamsburg, while the general "marketing" category totaled $56,908 in addition.

A similar pattern emerges at Success Academy Cobble Hill. As at the Williamsburg campus, student recruitment was in the top five of Cobble Hill's greatest expenses in this year, although it occupied the third rather than the second slot (Table 3.7). In this case, more was spent on the management fee—possibly paid to the Success Academy organization. Again, however, these data do not include the amount spent on teacher recruiting ($58,882) or on general "marketing ($58,709) in that time period at Success Academy Cobble Hill.

"YOU CAN TELL A LOT ABOUT AN ORGANIZATION'S PRIORITIES": REFLECTIONS ON EDVERTISING BUDGETS

As stated earlier, budgets are reflective of organizational values and priorities. Although each of the regions reviewed in the case study is distinct in multiple ways, from our analysis we can see several overarching trends.

First, it appears that charter schools are leading the way in edvertising spending. Although it can be argued that many of these schools are new, and therefore need to establish their presence in their cities, or that they are not imbedded in larger political and organizational structures, such as districts and unions, upon whose resources they can draw, the fact that we see more consistent investment in marketing from charters is telling.

To a degree, it can be argued that you get the behaviors that you incentivize. Charters live more directly in quasi-market systems, and are therefore incentivized to engage in that market in a manner that perhaps traditional public schools are not. Engaging in any market requires information distribution. However, expenditures of the amounts we see here with KIPP DC or Success Academy constitute a significantly heavier investment than simply sending a neighborhood notice—this is about the management of messaging.

Second, it seems that in several of these regions, CMOs are outspending their non-network charter peers on edvertising. We see the stark contrast in the Massachusetts analysis, in particular. In some cases, local CMOs, like Excel in Massachusetts or Success Academy in New York City, are making major investments in edvertising. This may be due to a perceived need to grab a "share of voice" in order to compete on a larger scale with major brand leaders, like KIPP. This pattern raises questions about organizational economies of scale and sustainability: As current players in the market scale up, will they crowd out new voices of innovation by virtue of their advantage in grabbing share of voice? Questions can also be raised about the role that private investments are playing in supporting the edvertising practices.

More simply, however, the investment in edvertising itself is a finding. As noted in Chapter 2, several years ago the edvertising industry did not exist, per se. Yet today, not only do we see charter schools and networks securing executive teams to manage marketing and branding, but we find consistent, and oftentimes increasing, allocations of funding toward edvertising activities. However, it is of note that we do not see anywhere near the amount spent at traditional public schools or district offices—many of which do not have a marketing expenditure line item in their budgets. This echoes the findings in Chapter 2, where New York City Department of Education executives indicated that they do not feel pressure to "sell" their schools.

In considering this investment, we return to our economic theory of goods framework. To invest in something denotes an organizational belief in its value. Using the budgets of Success Academy as an example, one could reasonably infer from the high-ranked placement of recruiting that, organizationally speaking, edvertising practices are of more value than instructional supplies and textbooks when establishing a new school.

This returns us to our consideration of the ethical dilemmas that arise from edvertising. We must raise questions about the direction of the goals and purposes of public educational institutions that value image management of a school or network over educational supports, such as supplies. We contend that this values shift is indicative of the unintentional incentive structures created by today's market-like policies in schools. These budgets indicate that investments in edvertising must successfully yield consumer demand, in the form of applications and enrollment. In the case of CMOs, such as Success Academy, this demand is then the centerpiece of the organization's further argument to New York City to expand the school network. Thus, the edvertising investment creates manufactured demand, which reinforces the survival of the network itself.

Finally, we respect that these budgets are frustratingly incomplete, inconsistent, and self-reported. They do not represent the investments of all the schools in the region, nor of the larger management organizations. Marketing expenditures are often inconsistently labeled. This lack of transparency and accountability in budgeting for charter schools raises problematic ethical questions.

CHAPTER 4

The Activities of Edvertising
Traditional and Digital Advertisements

In this chapter we describe strategic initiatives: the tactics of edvertising used by educational organizations. We discuss the tools that CMO and district executives, introduced in Chapter 2, use to raise brand awareness and reach their target audiences. Adding to the budgetary allocation data discussed in Chapter 3, we highlight activity-specific costs as well as weigh the advantages and disadvantages of various edvertising pursuits. We conclude the chapter with a discussion of the ethical tensions that emerge as a result of these branding and marketing activities.

Data for this chapter come from the exploratory case study of branding and marketing practices in New York City, the methodology for which is reviewed in Chapter 2. We selected New York City because of its 10-year history with public school choice, as well as its robust charter sector. New York City is also the headquarters of many leading branding and marketing firms in the United States. Methods of data collection included documents and interviews. We collected information about marketing firms and advertising services and fees from a review of organizations' websites as well as interviews with sales executives from various media outlets, including radio, newspaper, direct mail, digital media, and outdoor advertising. We also analyzed branded artifacts such as branding manuals produced by advertising firms for educational organizations.

BRANDING AND MARKETING: THE CASE OF NEW YORK CITY

In New York City, approaches to branding and marketing, and the tools and channels employed therein, vary tremendously. Some organizations hire creative and advertising firms, while others do it in-house. Some use traditional print and media such as radio, while others use only digital. This section introduces the spectrum of branding and marketing practices used by the NYC DOE and CMOs in New York City. It highlights the breadth of practices employed by educational organizations, the strengths and drawbacks of each approach, and the role of targeting particular school populations.

Building a Brand

In line with the literature discussed in Chapter 1, all interviewees reported brand-building as the first step in developing a public image. Building a brand is a multi-step process. It begins with setting an organization's mission and vision, and ends with introducing that brand—through visual signifiers (e.g., logos, school uniforms) and targeted advertising campaigns targeted at specific communities and/or audiences. Interviewees reported taking various approaches to creating a brand—but all conveyed it involved developing a strong school mission and then creating a visual representation of it. A brand manager at a marketing firm shared their process:

> We engaged the schools that were open in 2011 in a conversation around what type of mark they would most like for their schools. It quickly became clear in conversations with school leadership, with focus groups of students, that they really wanted to have a pre-collegiate, college-preparatory, very academic-looking mark that they could really rally behind. After we had settled on a new visual design for [CMO name], we took those style standards, we brought on board a freelancer to help us figure out how we might create a crest using the same color palette as the [CMO] logo, and we developed the crest, which the schools have all adopted. My understanding is even though this is now 4 or 5 years in, they very much like using the crest. If you go visit the schools, some of the schools, you can see the crest everywhere. It's on door signs. It's on banners. Some of them use it on things like stationery letterhead. That became a signifier for the individual schools.

Upon creation of the visual brand, schools usually choose or are encouraged to place the visual signifiers "everywhere"—on banners, stationery, uniforms, to name just a few examples.

In organizations with highly orchestrated campaigns, the visual signifier is just one piece of their larger efforts. Many national CMOs have full branding manuals. These are 20- to 30-page documents, sometimes also referred to as "style guides," which outline in great depth all aspects of the visual brand. This includes which symbols can be used and when, color schemes, typeset and font sizes, and even wording guidelines for correspondence with families, teachers, and funders. Often, there is a section with guidance for social media use, as well as rules about interactions with media sources.

These manuals are part of an effort by CMOs to enforce adherence to a central brand identity, across sometimes geographically disparate school sites. As mentioned in Chapter 2, many of the CMOs that have these manuals also have teams from their central marketing office that visit schools to audit compliance to the branded image. Some of the manuals also come with catalogues to ensure compliance; to stay "on brand," schools must buy all of their branded items (uniforms, signs) from the CMO-sponsored catalogue.

Branding manuals, according to a leading nonprofit marketing firm in New York City, cost between $20,000 and $50,000 to produce. Pricing depends on the size of the manual and number of pictures present, and does not include printing. Across CMOs and the NYC DOE, all marketing personnel reported aspiring to the development of a branding manual for their respective organization, but often cited the prohibitive cost and time investment as reason for not having developed full-fledged manuals. Generally, only national CMOs such as KIPP Academy Public Schools and Achievement First had the financial means to create these full branding manuals.

CMOs and NYC DOE representatives, when pressed for particular challenges they face in building strong brands, cited two distinct themes. In the case of CMOs, it was how to create a coherent brand across a disjointed educational network. Some CMOs consist of a network of schools all with their own existing identities, and sometimes even brands. While the charter organizations did not want schools to lose the currency of their already developed individual brand awareness, they were interested in forging a larger, national identity. Introducing some uniformity was a worthwhile trade-off for the chance of being recognized as a national school reform contender.

In contrast, an official at the NYC DOE expressed frustration at the political nature of branding in New York—specifically, that signage and letterhead often had to have the names of key agencies and officials. He shared, "the City [brand] trumps the DOE. You had the Parks Department and the City brand and they both had to be there. But really that was to me always linking back to the politics of it because you know you will also have the mayor's name, the commissioner's name, and the election to come up. So there are those tensions." He continued to share that in an organization as large as the NYC DOE, it is very hard to have all stakeholders on the same page in terms of a singular branded image. The NYC DOE, citing capacity and cost, does not have a branding manual.

Direct Mail

Once the brand has been created, the next steps in the process involve production and dissemination. Direct-mail companies play an integral role in this process, as they hold the proverbial keys to the castle: student addresses. Direct mail is one of the most common ways for CMOs, districts, and individual schools to get their message out to the public. Direct mail consists of postcards, letters, fliers, and brochures that a designated company mails directly to families. Because of the Family Educational Rights and Privacy Act (FERPA), students' privacy must be protected. In New York, to protect students while giving organizations access to market to them, the district contracts with a direct-mail organization that holds all of the addresses of NYC public school children. An executive for a leading direct-mail service in New York described the relationship: "We have a confidentiality agreement with the DOE. We do not give the student name and addresses out, what we manage is the actual mailing side of it." Confirming this statement, all participants reported that in New York they had to "buy the list" from a direct-mail firm to get access to New York City's students.

Across the district and CMOs, directors reported using direct mail as a key component of their marketing plan. For charter schools, in particular, the use of direct mail increased 6 weeks prior to the charter school application deadline. A director of marketing at a national CMO shared: "Depending on the time of year, we do postcards directly to families that are within certain zip codes of our schools." Some CMOs send the school application directly to families, with return envelopes, as part of the marketing campaign to drive enrollment. A sales executive at a leading direct-mailing firm in New York City shared that charter schools dominate the direct-mail market: "I'm talking mostly to the charter schools because they're the ones who are reaching out to the marketing arena. Most of the Department of Education work for the school is their own internal documents." She went on to explain that the external documents were often professional development materials for administrators and teachers. In contrast to this more pedagogically oriented work, she shared that competitive pressure among charters to market their schools was intense.

One problem with direct-mail campaigns is ineffective consumer targeting—since the only available information is students' names and addresses. When CMOs and schools want to target particular populations or a specific gender, decisions rest on the perceived ethnic origins of a student's last name or the perceived gender associated with the first name. The marketing director at a national CMO shared these challenges: "The other thing that's sometimes trying about it is that for the bilingual mailer, we're trying to hit Spanish-speaking homes, but there's no way to do that besides last names. Nobody has a magic solution there." To avoid this problem, some CMOs send mailings in multiple languages.

The biggest expense associated with direct mail is postage. Most direct mail goes first class. In New York City, according to a leading direct-mail company, the average cost per student/family including postage is between 65 cents and $1 each. In terms of reach, in New York, lists range from 750 to 18,000 names. A sales executive at the same firm shared that "[n]ot everybody's doing the same thing, and not everybody has the same budget, and not everybody has the same number of families they're reaching out to. Some of the charter schools in Harlem have very hard, big numbers, but if you go out to Queens or Staten Island, you're looking at like smaller communities." As the executive suggests, charter schools located in areas with high levels of school competition are spending more on direct mailing. This finding, as well as other indicators, suggests a particular interest in certain highly competitive neighborhoods, such as Harlem, the South Bronx, and parts of Central Brooklyn.

THE ACTIVITIES OF EDVERTISING: TRADITIONAL AND DIGITAL

Once the brand has been created and outreach materials have been distributed, the next step is advertising. Advertising is generally divided into two categories: traditional and digital. Advertising in newspapers, on the radio, and outdoors are key components of traditional media.

Newspapers

Traditionally, newspaper advertising consists of print advertisements, usually printed in black and white. Advertisements can come in many sizes, ranging from a 1-inch column to a whole page. Increasingly, newspapers have either moved to completely digital platforms, or have a digital component. From an advertising perspective, digital advertising, as is discussed later in this chapter, allows for more targeted advertising. It also allows for integration with larger social media applications, such as Facebook.

A strength of newspaper advertising rests in its ability to target communities by geographic location or language/ethnic identity. For example, in New York City, while the *Daily News* or the *New York Post* circulate citywide, papers such as the *Brooklyn Courier* or *Queens Ledger* can target specific neighborhoods. Additionally, other newspapers target specific language/ethnic groups, such as *The Haitian Times* or *El Diario New York*. Directors of marketing at both CMOs and the NYC DOE reported using both citywide and local newspapers to reach the public. CMOs tended to use newspapers to advertise their schools and schools' lotteries. In contrast, the NYC DOE used newspaper advertising to tell the public about an array of educational programs, from school lunch to universal pre-K.

Directors of marketing cited cost as a drawback to newspapers. A NYC DOE official shared: "I mean four pages in the *Daily News,* in *Metro New York,* and *El Diario.* I don't know if it was like 60 grand a month." The director at a national CMO shared: "We haven't done student advertising in traditional print. We just haven't found it to be a huge driver. I know Success Academies [Charter Schools] does it. I'm sure others do it too. I think budget is one reason why we don't." A newspaper sales executive at a leading daily paper shared that local educational organizations are given the lowest rates. She says that "the average cost of a full page, it's gone down as circulation has gone down; it's gone down but it's between $7,500 and $10,000 for a full-page ad." To this end, a half-page ad run for 1 day would be

$5,000, while a quarter-page ad would be $2,500. The executive explained that frequency plays a key role in rates. Specifically, if an ad is to be run over a series of weeks, the daily rate drops; see Table 4.1 for specific figures. Interestingly, in terms of cost, New York City has longstanding contracts with various news outlets that offer legacy pricing and other discounts.

Even though marketing directors cited cost as a deterrent, the majority of charter school marketing executives reported running advertisements in newspapers, in particular community newspapers, 6 weeks prior to charter school lotteries. As one director of marketing shared: "We've also done things like advertising either in community newspapers or we've even done a bus shelter advertisement . . . we'll usually run for 4 or 6 weeks prior to the lottery, just as a further means of getting the word out that the school is opening and that it's accepting applications."

Radio

Similar to newspapers, radio advertising has evolved to include digital as well. Radio advertising might integrate traditional commercials, on-air personalities, and music festival tie-ins as well as access to digital radio platforms. Or it could simply be a series of radios commercials on a particular station.

Digital radio, which consists of mobile applications and websites, is an increasingly popular medium on which companies advertise. Radio websites, like other digital content, can offer customers banner ads, whole-page takeovers, and videos to engage the audience in a particular topic. Digital affords the ad buyer valuable information about the effectiveness of an advertisement. A director of radio sales explained: "With digital, you can track it because we have what we call digital performance reports. . . . I can tell you how many impressions, how many people that you're reaching, and also how many clicks, how many times they clicked on your particular ad. That's trackable, and that can show whether it's a success on this one thing."

One of the strengths of radio is the ability to target groups of people who follow a particular station. The director of sales at a leading radio company described how radio stations can be segmented by listener age as well as by racial and ethnic identity.

While none of the directors of marketing of CMOs interviewed for the study reported using radio to advertise, the NYC DOE reported using radio, most notably for the rolling out of the 2014 universal pre-K initiative in New York City. The goal of the campaign was to inform parents about the program and enrollment deadlines.

Radio is expensive. Campaigns range from $20,000 to $300,000, depending on the exposure (commercials, music festivals, etc.) and length of the campaign. To put this in perspective, $20,000 would buy a 2-week campaign

Table 4.1. Cost and Reach of Traditional Edvertising

Traditional Media Outlet	Services	Cost	Purchaser	Audience	Targeted?
Radio	Campaign with on-air messaging, and desktop banner ads, for 2 weeks, citywide	$20,000	NYC DOE	Parents and teachers	No
Radio	Integrated campaign with radio personalities, digital and connections to music festivals, for 12 weeks, citywide	$300,000	n/a	n/a	No
Newspaper (major)	One page ad, for 1 day, citywide	$7,500	NYC DOE	Parents	No
Newspaper (major)	One page ad, runs for 1 day	$1,600	NYC DOE	Parents	Yes
Outdoor Media	318 buses, for 4 weeks, citywide	$130,000	NYC DOE, CMOs	Parents and teachers	No
Outdoor Media	Buses with bus-stop panels for 4 weeks	$50,000	NYC DOE, CMOs	Parents and teachers	Yes
Outdoor Media	1,000 20-by-21-inch subway ads for 4 weeks	$50,000	NYC DOE, CMOs	Parents	Yes

with on-air and desktop banner ads, while $300,000 would buy a 12-week integrated campaign with radio ads and personalities, digital ads, as well as promotions at various music festivals. In terms of NYC contracts, anything below $25,000 does not require official bidding or vetting processes.

Outdoor

Outdoor, or out-of-home, advertising consists of ads on subways, buses, billboards, urban panels, and street furniture (for example, bus shelters). Outdoor advertising can blanket an entire area or be targeted to reach particular geographic locations.

Frequency and reach are key levers of outdoor advertising. Frequency refers to how often a consumer sees the ad. The power of frequency is that, over time, it contributes to brand-building. Reach refers to the amount of people who can experience the advertisement. In describing the reach of outdoor advertising, an executive at a leading outdoor media firm shared: "On the subway, you're reaching just by the size of New York City, you're reaching close to 6 million riders a day. . . . There's enough people on the subway that they can be the trend initiators to sign up your kid for classes, or afterschool classes, or go to a library program." He goes on to explain the power of outdoor media to shape consumer behavior and preferences: "Basically the whole brilliant thing is, you increase awareness, you change perceptions, and then you influence behavior, and that takes time. The subway is unique regarding how that. . . . It does it, because you're spending so much time down there, right?"

The goal of outdoor media is to fully cover, or saturate, a marketplace, usually involving a combination of subways, buses, and street furniture. Time also plays a role. Specifically, the longer an ad runs, the more likely it will become embedded in consumers' personal schema. An executive at a leading outdoor media firm explained: "Like on the buses now, you might not have a kid, or the kid might be one or two, and not ready yet, and I don't think that . . . I've expressed that to Success Academy and other people, I don't think people realize it, right? I think your brain needs time to put that away, and keep it as a mental note, right? There's an immediacy thing, and then there's a brand-building thing." Brand-building is all about increasing consumer's trust in a product—in this case, a school. This is particularly important in education when a person's need for the product—that is, a school—changes over time and life circumstances (Ackerberg, 2001; Silk, 2006).

In New York City, both the district and national charter organizations use outdoor media. NYC DOE's campaigns tend to focus on public service messaging—for example, multilingual accessibility in NYC public schools and universal pre-K programs. These campaigns are citywide and use a combination of subway, bus, and street furniture formats. Some programs, such as the summer free-lunch program, are targeted more to high-poverty areas of the city, including parts of upper Manhattan, the South Bronx, and central Brooklyn. To reach these areas, subway and bus routes would be targeted for advertising.

CMOs also use outdoor media. More market-driven in their messages, the CMOs advertise for enrollment purposes. The advertisements are also targeted to particular communities. When talking about his work with a leading national CMO, an outdoor media executive explained: "They're specific to literally, I mean, we'll have the conversations, and it's like, 'We just want to be in these zip codes.'" He further explained:

> You put together the mapping of all their zip codes. We have enough bus coverage that covers these zip codes. There's some leakage, but at the end of the day, we know that even though you don't live in those zip codes, or the school's not in the zip code, people travel that live in those zip codes, or go to school that travel outside those zip codes, so it's going to be a win-win. We're doing a lot of buses for [the National CMO] in regards to that. We also did street furniture and place-based urban panels. All that together works.

Outdoor media pricing varies by a customer's goals for reach and frequency—how many people they're trying to reach and how often they want the ad to be viewed. Citywide campaigns tend to be more expensive than targeted campaigns, with the exception of certain premium areas such as Times Square. Cost also depends on the level of saturation being targeted in a given campaign. Further, some campaigns are generally packaged as "showings" campaigns, which the NYC DOE tends to favor because they run cheaper. On the other hand, CMOs targeting a particular area would purchase "special" packages, which are specifically targeted (area, demographic) and tend to be pricier. Finally, price is influenced by the size of the contract and the length of time an organization has been a client. New York City, for example, has a longstanding contract with prominent outdoor advertising firms.

Digital

Digital advertising is the most flexible of all advertising, in both form and pricing. It is also easily measured, allowing buyers to understand the net impact of their ads. The two most common forms of digital advertising are paid word-search ads and display ads.

Paid word-search ads are most often associated with (and found on) search engines, such as Google. Advertisers pay to have their ads displayed to users who search for particular items, come from specific demographic backgrounds, or espouse specific behaviors. While paid search words can help particular organizations pop up first when a search is conducted, organizational type and size also affects the display of results. For example, with Google Adwords, government ".gov" designations get first showing in the results display—a clear plus for district-run schools. Google Adwords also offers a grant program to nonprofits, giving them an allotted amount of free ad dollars. The one caveat is the ads cannot be used for school recruitment. A director of marketing at a CMO reported using this grant program to advertise for open faculty or administrative positions, but not for students.

Display ads, also known as banner ads, can take up a whole screen or part of a screen. They can be text, images, video, or a combination of formats. These ads can be found on social media platforms such as Facebook or Instagram, but also on newspaper and radio websites, as mentioned earlier. These ads can be targeted to people based on their demographics (age, race, income, location), behaviors (buying patterns, browsing history), and retargeting (tracking past visitors to your site). Browsers can click on the display, which then takes them directly to the organization or company's website. It is this ability to "click" that allows both for the impact of the ad to be measured and also for the company to collect the browsing history of the user.

Directors of marketing for CMOs and the NYC DOE reported display ads to be their preferred means of reaching consumers. In particular, they cited leveraging display ads on Facebook to be very effective. The director of marketing at a national CMO shared: "For student recruitment, it's primarily just Facebook ads. You can pick a group of people. You can be like, 'I would like to target 20- to 30-year-old women in Bridgeport who have an interest in children' or something other than that that signifies that they have kids. Then they will see that ad." Similarly, the director of marketing at the NYC DOE reported that display ads were effective and cost efficient. He shared: "We see a big impact from Facebook ads; a majority of our audience is on Facebook. So our engagement rates are upwards usually 3 to 4%."

Directors of marketing showed a preference for display ads over other more traditional types of media because of their cost, reach, and measurable impacts; see Table 4.2 for specific amounts. The director of marketing at a national CMO explained: "The answer is that you can set your budget as whatever you want. You can be like, 'I'm going to pay $100 for this.' It's done by impressions basically. You can do an ad for as little as 10 bucks. The amount of money that the ad costs you is dependent on how many people see it. It's not like you throw up a billboard, and you're like 'I paid two grand for this billboard. I hope somebody looks at it.'"

Costs across many media platforms—including digital, radio, newspaper, and outdoors—are calculated by cost-per-thousand (CPM), which measures the cost of an ad per 1,000 impressions or displays. Across many digital and social media platforms, the ad consumer sets a maximum price, which in turn determines how many people will be exposed to the ad. This budget can be adjusted depending on a given organization's desire for

Table 4.2: Cost and Reach of Digital Edvertising

Digital Media	Services	Cost	Purchaser	Audience	Targeted?
Social Media Banner Ads	Pop-up advertisements on social media	$1,850 to $5,000/ month per channel depending on size and complexity	CMOs	Parents and teachers	Yes
Search Engine Ads	Google "Adwords"	Average cost per click: $1–2	CMOs	Parents and teachers	Yes
Display Ads	Impressions	$1.00 for every 1,000 impressions	NYC DOE, CMOs	Parents and teachers	Yes
	Clicks on ads	Range: .01 to $1 per click with retargeting	NYC DOE, CMOs	Parents and teachers	Yes

visibility. A second cost measure, in digital, is click-through rate (CTR). The CTR is determined by the number of times the targeted audience clicks on an impression. CTR is one way of measuring the success of a campaign. Given the reach of the ads, as well as the flexibility in form and pricing, it is not surprising that digital media are popular for educational advertising.

EDVERTISING IN THE BIG APPLE: A PRIMER FOR "HOW TO" TARGET SPECIFIC POPULATIONS

This chapter has described how branding and marketing, hallmarks of the corporate sector, are being used in the public education sector. It captured the breadth and depth of branding and marketing practices across New York City. It also illustrated the costs—financial and personnel—associated with these practices. A key finding from the data is that in New York City the use of branding and marketing in public education is not evenly distributed. The organizations that used the most sophisticated branding and marketing practices were the NYC DOE central offices and large CMOs. Individual NYC public schools and autonomous charter schools might embrace aspects of marketing and branding, but did not engage in orchestrated campaigns due to cost and personnel capacity.

While the CMOs and the NYC DOE were the key players, their intentions differed. CMOs' campaigns were more market driven, while the NYC DOE's campaigns were more civic oriented. CMOs tended to focus both on brand-building and marketing. These organizations allocated key resources to creating a strong and distinguishable brand—to make them stand out from their competitors within both the charter and traditional school arenas. Speaking to Smith's research (1956) on segmentation, these organizations also tended to target geographic locations, such as the South Bronx or Harlem, where new charter schools were opening, or in existing charter school locations if there was a perceived need to increase school enrollment. Since funding is directly linked to student enrollment, the perception is that more marketing equals more enrolled students and, in turn, more money. This is why a sales executive working in direct mail, newspapers, and outdoor media reported a surge in advertising the 6 weeks before the charter school applications are due.

A director of marketing at a national CMO expressed some frustration at the bad press that charter schools receive about their more market-driven branding and marketing practices. Describing pushback regarding the organizations' direct mailer, she shared:

> Something that gets me every year has just happened to us on Twitter is that somebody gets our mailer that hates us. Some vehement anti-charter person gets our mailer, puts it online, or waves it around at a meeting and says, "the charter school is saying that they don't get the same funds as district schools," which is true by the way in [a northeastern state]. "Yet they can produce this beautiful mailer. I'm mad about it." For me, that's always tough to take because it's like the other criticism that charter schools get is that we just open our doors and only the most engaged parents come, and then we say, "Great, we just creamed the list." We have to do mailers, and we have to do fliers. Our community engagement people, they take those fliers and they go to every public housing complex that's near one of our schools. I feel like because we don't have what a district has, which is just we get every kid in this catchment area, we have to have a robust campaign to recruit students. Otherwise, we are having bias for only the most engaged families.

Here, the marketing executive argues that marketing to families prevents "creaming" and works to engage a spectrum of parents. Further, she posits that because charter schools do not automatically "get" students from particularly catchment areas—they must work harder than their district counterparts. While her perceptions are on target about the existing brand of community schools—both positive and negative—there is a difference between outreach to families about their new schools and highly orchestrated and financed ad campaigns.

In contrast, the NYC DOE's campaigns tended to be more civic oriented; they focused on raising awareness about a particular offering or program, such as universal pre-K or free school lunch. A large and known organization, NYC DOE did not need to spend resources on building its brand or introducing itself to the community. The director of marketing at the NYC DOE explained: "Communications from the government agent should be about the government serving the people, making government work." He went on: "In the City you know we're the opposite of a typical marketer; we're not looking at people with the highest disposable income but the lowest." While public sentiments might be mixed about the NYC DOE, they are an "experienced" and known entity, which gives their brand an established appeal to many parents (Silk, 2006). Additionally, the NYC DOE's, and for that matter, New York City's, longstanding relationship plus existing contracts with particular companies affords them more competitive pricing. It is also important to note that since the NYC DOE tends to reach out to all students, the broad scale of their marketing needs also gives them leverage when negotiating price.

Across all organizations, digital, direct mail, newspaper, and outdoor media were the most popular vehicles to get a message to the public. In particular, digital's competitive pricing, targeted reach, and measurable outcomes—such as number of clicks on a particular ad—made it very appealing across all organizations. Direct-mail companies also featured prominently. The direct-mail firm with its NYC DOE contracts controlled access to all students' addresses. It is not surprising that it reported a boon in educational marketing practices over the past 10 years. It is also not surprising that executives working for the leading direct-mail firm in New York City could name the regions of the city with the most competitive school choice markets. This desire to target specific neighborhoods or communities made newspaper and outdoor advertising appealing because they allowed for a physical saturation of a particular niche market, be it in the case of a language group with the newspaper or in a geographic area with bus and bus shelter ads. Compared to digital, of course, the drawback of these approaches is their cost.

It is clear from the data presented in this chapter that branding and marketing practices are on the rise in New York City, and a result it is essential to weigh the ethical implications of these practices. This embrace of branding and marketing brings a new language, set of products, and strategies to New York City's public schools. While some schools successfully compete in this arena with their glossified campaigns, others, particularly smaller public and charter schools, do not have the knowledge of branding and marketing or the resources to compete. Given that edvertising is a relatively recent phenomenon within public education, how are policy-makers and district leaders, alike, making sense of these inequities across a singular school system? From a systems perspective, who is taking stock of these changes in communication and outreach? These queries build on the findings in Chapters 2 and 3, raising ethical questions about the increased influence of branding and marketing on personnel decisions and on school finance, respectively.

Parents' and students' experiences of branding and marketing vary; certain parent communities—often high-poverty communities of color—are targeted much more than others. In these highly competitive marketing hot-beds, families are bombarded with branding and marketing at literally every corner—or bus stop. Reflecting on Weick's (1995) work: How are these parents (and older students) making sense of being the targeted consumers within these highly marketized environments? Where are they within the sensemaking processes? Are they actors absorbing (enacting) the marketing messages, or are they reflecting on their own place and space within this larger choice environment? Parents, many of whom work full-time, must sift through a muddle of often incomplete information to make the best possible decision for their child. What impact does branding and marketing have on parental decisionmaking, and what are the ethical implications for public education?

CHAPTER 5

Perceptions of Prestige
An Analysis of Digital Marketing

In highly competitive school markets such as New York City, New Orleans, and Boston, the effort to distinguish via marketing occurs not only among schools, but also among school management organizations. Schools and organizations employ marketing campaigns to compete for families, faculty, and funding.

Reflecting back on the literature regarding advertising and marketing from the business world, we see how a consumer's perception of the monetary investment in particular marketing campaigns (such as social media) and advertising outlets (such as websites) transmutes into a perception of quality (Ackerberg, 2001). This supports the supposition that marketing is meeting its goal of conveying the value of the "good" of a particular school or organization to consumers, be they parents, students, or potential backers (Menger, 1976).

As shown in previous chapters, these perceptions are propelled by actual investment in edvertising campaigns. Many CMO-managed charters have their own proprietary marketing teams that develop consistent branding identities for the organization and for individual schools. In fact, as mentioned earlier, CMOs such as Achievement First and KIPP have entire pages of their organizational website dedicated to brand identity management. This type of organization structure requires a material monetary investment for, at minimum, staff salaries.

As Chapter 4 highlighted, digital marketing is becoming an increasingly popular marketing tactic and advertising investment area. In this chapter we take a deep dive into the practices and processes involved with online marketing. Focusing again on the primary purpose of the book—capturing the landscape of edvertising practices across key fields of organization—we further unpack the use and impact of new technology in advancing organizational messages.

While earlier studies looked at traditional educational marketing mechanisms, such as school brochures (Lubienski, 2007; Symes, 1998) and, more recently, websites (Drew, 2013; Hernandez, 2016; Wilkins, 2012), this chapter additionally includes an exploration of social media platforms—Facebook, Twitter, and YouTube. By conducting a document evaluation of websites and social media platforms from a variety of school types in several districts across the nation, we examine the quality of the content of marketing and branding occurring in these outlets. Distinctions are drawn not only between types of schools, but also between the ways in which schools market different "qualities" of their educational institution.

This chapter finds, in particular, that CMO charter schools are engaging in "prestige" rather than "informational" marketing. In prestige marketing, the quality of a product is conveyed in part based on the viewer's perception of the amount of money being spent on the marketing campaign (Ackerberg, 2001). The goal is to directly shape consumer perceptions through investments in online content such as websites, YouTube videos, and social media campaigns. Additionally, different messages can be targeted to different sets of consumers. In this case, we argue that prestige marketing campaigns are being applied to appeal not just to parents and students, but also to potential wealthy donors. Ultimately, the efficacy of this approach contributes to inequities between schools that have access to greater sources of marketing capital and strategic support.

Existing research on the performance of CMO charter schools is mixed (Shah, 2011). Yet CMOs have continued to proliferate around the country, garnering public grants and policy support (USDOE, 2012), raising financial capital through venture philanthropy streams, and attracting students and parents. Further, as seen in New York City, school partner organizations and/or management organizations are electing to follow the same path as CMOs. This suggests a broadly held perception that funding and prestige follow the CMO model. Given Ackerberg's (2001) theory, one can question the degree to which this perception is a direct result of the investment these CMOs have put toward marketing campaigns aimed at a variety of stakeholders.

This leads to a bigger question about the underlying purpose of marketing campaigns. In mimicking the private sector in marketing campaigns, CMOs might be attempting to convey the value of their model, or charters in general, not primarily to the parent public but rather to investors from the private sector (Menger, 1976). With the investment of venture philanthropy, CMOs can continue to operate and replicate models across the country. In this situation, marketing goes beyond influencing intangible perceptions and starts to influence the makeup of schooling "markets" themselves.

This chapter raises important questions about the implications of building quasi-educational marketplaces. Given the current federal government pro-choice education agenda, it is possible that states will lift their charter caps and embrace pro-choice and voucher legislation. This will increase school choice and, as research shows, likely increase branding and marketing practices at the district—CMO and public—and school level (Jabbar, 2016a; Jessen & DiMartino, 2016; Lubienski, 2005). As districts and schools compete to tell their stories—using various social media platforms and outlets—those with access to greater financial resources will have an advantage in their ability to capture a share of the market voice in an impactful, coherent way. This form of competition creates a situation likely to further stratify an already segregated and segmented education system.

MESSAGING "SCHOOLS" IN THE AGE OF TWITTER

The data for this case come from publicly available online content, primarily consisting of websites, social media campaigns, and (where applicable) YouTube videos from 50 schools in two metro areas (Boston and New York City). School websites and social media are key sources of marketing and advertising today—not just for parents, but also for the broader public. In addition to online media being one of the primary ways of reaching the public today, various degrees of online presence can be established by schools beyond traditional websites, including social media and YouTube channels. We look for the presence and quality of these as well.

Within these metro areas, schools were selected based on their school type, location, and the meeting of certain criteria (Table 5.1). For example, charter schools were grouped into charter schools belonging to networks or managed by CMOs versus autonomous charter schools. They were then further subdivided into schools in urban and suburban locations—as were the noncharter public schools. Noncharter public schools were additionally subdivided by whether or not they were schools of choice. For each subcategory, two schools within the metro area were selected and reviewed. We also included local-area private schools in our review in order to compare content, as well as two examples of for-profit or new types of private educational management organizations, which will be discussed later.

Although these schools represent a small proportion of the institutions in these two metro areas, the selection of case schools, most notably of particular types, proved to be somewhat challenging. Because of the lack of CMO-affiliated charter schools in the suburbs, for example, or even "traditional" public schools in urban areas, many times our pool of school candidates was extremely limited. We also struggled with the definitions of "suburban" versus "urban," particularly as New York City and Boston have quite different geographical structures. In several instances, particularly in the case of charter or magnet schools, not enough schools were located in suburban locations. Often we found schools within these category types that might be considered to be in smaller metro areas of their own, located in the regions of Boston and New York City. For example, several of the suburban magnet schools in the Boston metro sample were located in Worcester, which is by definition a small city.

Also of note is that it became clear when taking a wide geographic sweep of these metro regions that schools of choice tend to be located in communities where student demographics show a lower-income and

Table 5.1. Number and Types of Selected Case Schools

School Category Type	Location	Organizational Type	Boston	New York
Charter School	Urban	CMO	Phoenix Charter Academy; Uncommon Schools, Roxbury Prep; KIPP Academy Boston; Match Academy Boston; Excel Academy Boston	Achievement First East New York; Success Academy Cobble Hill; Democracy Prep Charter High School
		Non-CMO	Codman Academy; Neighborhood House Charter School	Community Roots Charter School; Amber Charter School; University Prep Charter High School
	Suburban	CMO	KIPP Lynn Academy Collegiate; City on a Hill New Bedford	Leadership Prep Canarsie (Uncommon Schools)
		Non-CMO	Christa McAuliffe Charter School; Marblehead Community Charter School	Roosevelt Children's Academy Charter School; Evergreen Charter School
Public School of Choice (Non-Charter)	Urban	n/a	Eliot K8 Innovation School; Boston Teachers Union School; New Mission High School; Mission High School	The Urban Assembly New York Harbor School, MS 51; Astor Collegiate Academy; Bronx Aerospace High School
	Suburban	n/a	Chandler Magnet School; Worcester Arts Magnet School	Long Island High School for the Arts; Jack Abrams STEM Magnet School
"Traditional" Public Schhol	Urban	n/a	East Boston High; Charlestown High School	P.S. 005; P.S. 107; Truman High School
	Suburban	n/a	Wellesley High School; Framingham High School	Huntington High School; Dobbs Ferry High School
Private/ Independent School	Urban	n/a	Cambridge Friends School; Commonwealth School	The Spence School; Collegiate School
	Suburban	n/a	St. Mark's School; Concord Academy	Hackley School; Dwight-Englewood School
Other	Urban	For profit or privately managed	n/a	BASIS Private School

higher-non-White representation. In higher-income suburbs, for example, we found no shortage of traditional public schools and private schools from which to select for this sample. This is consistent with common assumptions about school segregation patterns, the literature on school choice, and is often the stated purpose of charter schools is to address inequities in regions of high need.

In addition, we tried where possible to vary the case selection by the CMO that managed the charter schools in each city in order to get a broader sweep of the landscape of CMO charters. In the case of more widely adopted national chains such as KIPP, this again limited our case selection. Finally, it is important to distinguish between the national and larger CMO brands and the smaller, more localized CMOs. In some cases, particularly with suburban CMO charters, these management organizations were operating four or five charters in the area, which technically classifies them as a CMO but does not put them on the same organizational scale as KIPP, for example.

Using the rubric we developed, websites were evaluated for the presence or degree of certain types of marketing or branding (Table 5.2). Rubric categories include the presence of mission statement, the presence of slogan, slogan language type (e.g., values, academic), the use of an autonomous website (i.e., not embedded within a district page), a "glossified" website (including high-resolution photos, videos, and flash or interactive graphics), the presence of social media campaigns, the existence of a school-owned YouTube channel, a branded school name including partner name or academic theme, and finally, a school name or mission statement with academic language cues.

These cases show that while variation exists within and across school type and location depending on the competitive nature of the school market in which it is located and the school's accompanying network or partner, overall, schools affiliated with high-status and well-funded organizations, such as the Success Academy, Urban Assembly, and KIPP networks, tend to have high-gloss websites and active social media outlets. In short, CMO charters are much more in control of their marketing message than other schools—even autonomous charter schools—and create a perception of "quality" through marketing.

Websites

Across the board, CMO charters present more prestige and outputs-oriented imagery. It is clear that an orchestrated marketing effort has been put into developing the website and corresponding materials, including social media content outlets (Table 5.3). Like the private schools in our case set, CMO-operated charter schools have websites with highly interactive graphics, glossy pictures, and high-quality videos. In more cases than all other school types, they also have logos, slogans, and mission statements.

Table 5.2. Rubric Categories and Data Descriptions

Online Source	Description		
Website	Presence of website?		
	Autonomously managed website		
	Flash graphics		
	High-resolution "glossy" pictures and graphics		
	Presence of logo		
	Presence of mission statement		
	Professional videos		
	Presence of slogan		
	School name that includes corporate or branded identity (example: KIPP or College Board)		
	School name that includes academic focus indicators (example: science)		
	School name that includes academic outcomes cues (example: "college" or "prep")		
	Visible school uniforms		
	Clear branded colors		
YouTube Channel	Autonomously managed YouTube channel		
	Professionally developed videos		
	Branded colors or logos present		
Social Media	Twitter	Existence of/autonomously managed	
		Branded colors/logos	
		Average number of followers	
	Facebook	Existence of/autonomously managed	
		Branded colors/logos	
		Average number of likes	

Interestingly, CMO charter schools in this data set commonly manage websites without giving individual schools their own, autonomous website. The individual schools were mostly embedded within the heavily branded, overarching CMO website. This gives the CMOs globally branded imagery that crosses geographic boundaries. For example, KIPP schools have the "KIPP" brand name in the title followed by the signifying colon and the regional name. They use a unifying blue coloring on their materials—from websites to uniforms. Success Academy uses orange coloring. These signify unity of vision and investment across schools in various local, regional, and national contexts.

Table 5.3. Website Analysis

	CMO Charters	Non-CMO Charters	Public Schools of Choice	Public Schools, Not Choice	Private Schools
Presence of website?	100%	100%	100%	100%	100%
Autonomously managed website	0%	100%	55%	55%	100%
Flash graphics	100%	40%	18%	11%	75%
High-resolution "glossy" pictures and graphics	100%	40%	18%	0%	88%
Presence of logo	100%	80%	45%	56%	88%
Presence of mission statement	100%	80%	55%	56%	88%
Professional videos	36%	10%	0%	0%	38%
Presence of slogan	100%	30%	9%	33%	33%
School name that includes corporate or branded identity (e.g., KIPP, College Board, or IB)	100%	0%	27%	0%	13%
School name that includes academic focus indicators (e.g., science)	0%	10%	55%	0%	0%
School name that includes academic outcome cues (e.g., "college" or "prep")	55%	10%	9%	0%	13%
Visible school uniforms	100%	40%	9%	0%	13%
Clear branded colors	100%	30%	27%	0%	25%
Average marketing score	76%	44%	33%	24%	52%

In contrast, traditional public and charter schools—in these markets that are not affiliated with networks or management organizations—had significantly less sophisticated websites. Picture quality, site design, and usability lagged behind their well-networked peers. More often than not, schools affiliated with districts would simply have a single webpage, perhaps with a logo or a mission statement, embedded within the district page. Autonomous charter schools commonly had their own websites, but with some notable exceptions these schools frequently had low- to medium-quality graphics and branding profiles.

The intensity of marketing tactics found on CMO charter websites echo those of elite private schools in interactive quality and imagery, but in contrast focus more on academic signals rather than values to sell their product (Lubienski, 2007). In New York City, for example, the Spence School, an elite private school, carries the slogan, "Not for school, but for life we learn." In contrast, local CMO-managed schools have more academic-oriented slogans; consider the Achievement First Public School chain, whose slogan is embedded in its name.

Using Lubienski's (2007) codes for marketing analysis, we see that the vast majority of CMO-operated charter schools focused heavily on academic themes, particularly college acceptance. Figure 5.1 illustrates these findings. Although all of the reviewed schools show some emphasis on academic language in their mission statements, CMO charters heavily emphasized such language. These mission statements were largely focused on "achievement" and "excellence," along with indicators of collegiate aspiration. Interestingly, none of the CMO charters mentioned "community" in their mission statements. For each of the other school types, "community" references were fairly consistent. Private schools, which had similarly comprehensive and invested marketing strategies as CMO charter schools, emphasized character more than other school types, echoing Lubienski's (2007) findings that private institutions focused more on values in their marketing literature. Finally, it is worth noting that although several schools mentioned "citizenship," for traditional public schools that are not of choice, "citizenship" was mentioned much more frequently in the mission statements. This is particularly significant given debates over the divergent goals of charter and noncharter schools within public education as a whole (Lubienski, 2005).

YouTube and Social Media

In addition to glossy websites, CMO charters have several other means of using online marketing and advertising to highlight their schools. Many CMO charters have high-quality, professionally developed, and emotionally appealing videos—often linked to a CMO-controlled YouTube channel. Table 5.4 shows the data from the YouTube channels of the case schools in this study. Although multiple schools throughout the sample had YouTube

Figure 5.1. Language of Mission Statement of Case Schools, by School Type

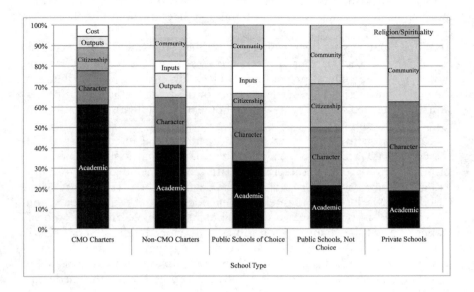

Table 5.4. YouTube Analysis

	CMO Charters	Non-CMO Charters	Public Schools of Choice	Public Schools, Not Choice	Private Schools
Autonomously managed YouTube channel	91%	26%	9%	11%	50%
Professionally developed videos	73%	0%	9%	0%	13%
Branded colors or logos present	82%	20%	9%	0%	38%
Average Marketing Score	82%	15%	9%	4%	33%

channels, many were unbranded, and most had videos posted by individual users of events, such as band concerts or graduations. CMO charters were much more intentionally organized and cohesive in the use of this media for marketing purposes. For example, Success Academies manages its own YouTube channel with over 130 videos. While some videos focus explicitly on the parent, teacher, or student experiences at Success Academy Schools, others are more general promotional videos highlighting the attributes of the organization as a whole. The majority of the videos appear to be professionally produced in quality; few are "homemade" uploads by members of the school community.

In addition to being indicative of organizational intention, such videos come with a clear financial price tag. Given that assumed price tag, surprisingly only one of the eight private schools included in this sample had a YouTube channel developed to the degree of the vast majority of the CMOs. St. Mark's School, an elite independent school, was the only non-CMO school in the sample to have the combination of an autonomously managed YouTube channel, professionally developed videos, and a clearly branded identity on that YouTube channel. This suggests that CMO charters are not only able to financially support such marketing enterprises, but that they are organizationally prioritizing marketing through this media in a way that mimics not private schools, but rather the corporate sector.

CMO charters are also extremely active within social media outlets such as Facebook and Twitter (Table 5.5). The CMO-managed charter schools were all linked to active Facebook and Twitter accounts, all of which were branded and showed consistent use. Chapter 2 gives us a window into the intention behind this strategy. In addition, many of these accounts make use of these platforms for political activism. For example, Success Academy and KIPP use the hashtag "#lovemycharter," which supports activism for charter schools in general. On the CMO social media sites, professionally developed videos often appear, some of which start up immediately when the user arrives at the account page. A few CMOs, such as Uncommon Schools and Achievement First, have also developed Instagram and Snapchat accounts, branded and managed in a manner akin to their other social media outlets.

In terms of number of followers and "likes," the CMO charters are far outstripping the other schools in this case sample. For example, KIPP Academy has over 17,000 followers on Twitter, and each individual school has its own account, with thousands of followers per school. The same is true for most of the CMO charter schools. Even the private schools, which follow the CMO charters in terms of degree of social media activity, have only a fraction of the followers.

This disparity can be partly attributed to the organizational structure of these types of institutions. CMO-managed charters, particularly the national ones, have an interest in using social media to give an impression of (and

Table 5.5. Social Media Analysis

		CMO Charters	Non-CMO Charters	Public Schools of Choice	Public Schools, Not Choice	Private Schools
Twitter account	Existence of/ autonomously managed	100%	30%	27%	22%	87%
	Branded colors/logos*	100%	100%	66%	50%	100%
	Average number followers*	**12, 653**	**123**	**815**	**93**	**938**
Facebook account	Existence of/ autonomously managed	100%	80%	90%	77%	100%
	Branded colors/logos*	100%	75%	50%	42%	87%
	Average number likes*	**12,042**	**640**	**714**	**1,928**	**1,429**

*Indicates case schools with accounts.

even create) cohesiveness across geographic boundaries, to recruit teachers from locations around the country, and, in theory, to reach parents outside of local neighborhoods. Yet, the number of followers for organizations such as KIPP indicates that some are reaching beyond the immediate parent and teacher community to a larger network of interested parties—including potential political and/or financial supporters (DiMartino, 2009).

While many of the traditional public and charter public schools in this sample have Facebook accounts, few are branded, and many are seemingly somewhat out of use. Some of these schools have Twitter accounts, most of which appear to exist to follow school sports teams. Overall, with the notable exception of Urban Assembly New York Harbor School, which has both Twitter and Facebook accounts that mimic the style of the CMO charters (albeit with fewer followers), the public schools in this sample do not give the impression of using these accounts for marketing so much as for community informational purposes. Interestingly, Urban Assembly, Harbor Schools' private-sector partner, recently announced it would begin operating charter schools in New York City. This provides yet another example of isomorphism in the field, as mentioned in Chapter 2.

The private schools in this sample were more likely than the public schools to have active social media accounts with branded identities. On many of these sites, however, it was clear that a significant portion of the activity was targeted at the alumni network for the schools. This returns us to the earlier statement about the reach of social media followers for CMO charters. In accessing alumni networks, private schools, in part, likely hope to maintain a feeling of connection among graduates, which ideally will translate into fundraising. A similar motivation is possibly true for CMO charters. In documenting activities and engaging in political activism through social media accounts, CMO charters are likely targeting potential donors as much as (or more than) maintaining parent and community ties.

Social media outlets as well as YouTube channels are frequently linked by color and logo branding back to their CMO. This relates back to consumer perceptions of a monetary investment in advertising. Each of these media outlets provides ample access to marketing materials, and in addition requires a staff member with some degree of technical skill and public relations knowledge to manage them. As Chapters 2 and 4 explain in depth, keeping social media sites current, information rich, and visually appealing is time-consuming and requires skilled personnel.

Additionally, we found that schools located in affluent, zoned neighborhoods, whether urban or suburban, had lower marketing indices. These schools already had distinguished brands tightly associated with their strong reputations as high-achieving schools. These reputations were associated with the elite communities themselves—because of high real estate prices or high tuitions—and often were touted by national publications such as *U.S. News and World Report*. The supposition is that their already established reputational identities perhaps mitigate the need for intensive marketing and branding practices.

INVESTED IN PRESTIGE

These cases return us to our economic value of goods. As Ackerberg (2001) indicates, schools with more invested in their websites, promotional videos, and social media outlets will be perceived as being of higher quality by parents, teachers, students, and investors.

Seemingly, the CMOs are leading this effort strategically. In this evaluation, we have seen how, overwhelmingly, CMO-run charter schools present a much glossier face in these online media outlets compared to other schools in the public sector. CMO websites are matched only in gloss by elite private schools, which are not accessible to all students and thus are targeting a different market segment. Many traditional and charter public schools project essentially no cohesive messaging. Rather, they rely on an informational or "constructive" approach (Marshall, 1919). Ergo, one can infer that the public perception of the quality of CMO charter schools is primed to be perceived as superior to other public schools or even autonomous charter schools, whether or not the actual performance matches that.

Interestingly, although the financial resources of exclusive private schools are likely greater than those of any public institution, even private schools are less noticeably aligned in their edvertising than charters. One might argue that this trend is a result of the ways in which charter networks are positioned in the market. Given the high degree of connection many of the CMO-led charter chains have to the business community and marketing executives, charter networks might simply be ahead of the curve in this field and possess the institutional know-how to execute an effective campaign.

However, we contend that this edvertising leadership among CMO-led charters is philosophically rooted. Beyond organizational ability, these cases illustrate strategic decisionmaking to invest in edvertising that we saw in Chapters 2 and 3. This reinforces the argument that these institutions view themselves as deeply integrated into the organizational field (Arum, 2000) of competitive educational market-like policies. These shifts raise ethical questions regarding the purposes of public education as represented via edvertising, and more specifically the impact of private-sector strategies on public education.

These cases also speak to the increasing diversity in the charter sector regarding management structure and scale, and potential alliances between autonomous charters and traditional public schools that previously might not have existed. We need future research to further investigate these relationships.

CHAPTER 6

Becoming the Organization

Teachers as Edvertising Actors

Both in our interviews with new marketing managers in Chapter 2 and our budget analysis in Chapter 3, we determined that a portion of money spent on edvertising is allocated for recruiting teachers. This trend is necessitated, in part, by the scale of the charter movement. Many large CMOs construct marketing campaigns to attract teachers to one unified brand from across the national landscape.

Teachers play a unique and understudied role in the landscape of edvertising. Not only are many teachers the target audience of marketing messages, but they also offer an exclusive perspective on the ways in which edvertising is enacted within schools with parents and students as targets. As organizational insiders who are generally removed from the immediate marketing decisionmaking that occurs at the management level, they are able to see and evaluate the brands, and the construction of organizational messages, perhaps better than any other actor in education today.

Teachers are active actors in many of the educational institutions we examine throughout this book. Our research indicates that they do more than play the role of target consumer of edvertising messages; often, they become active evangelists of organizational messaging. Thus, in this chapter we set out to examine how teachers interact, in various and nuanced ways, with edvertising.

Our research here examines a case of teachers in New Orleans. Teachers in this city tend to be imbedded not only in complex, citywide, market-like structures, but also within multiple, highly marketed organizations, such as CMOs and Teach for America (TEA). Existing research on marketing in New Orleans includes works by Jabbar (2015), which examined the role that principals play in the market-like system in the city, and found that they rely heavily on marketing techniques to expand their consumer base and compete with other schools. Our New Orleans case has implications about the implementation and outcomes of marketing practices in New Orleans from the perspective of teachers. In addition, it adds to the growing body of literature on edvertising by evaluating the role that Teach for America plays.

ON TEACHERS AND TEACH FOR AMERICA IN NEW ORLEANS

In Chapter 3 we reviewed some of the history and organizational structure of New Orleans after Hurricane Katrina. For this analysis, we augment that description to focus on context and teachers. Sims and Vaughn's (2014) review of student demographics in New Orleans reveals that while the overall school-age population in the city is 59.4% Black and 30.8% White, the public school composition is significantly more homogenous, with 85% of the student population identifying as Black.

Teacher demographics have changed dramatically since the hurricane, according to Babineau, Hand, and Rossmeier (2017). Before the hurricane, 71% of teachers in New Orleans were Black, whereas today, only 49% are Black. Today, 65% of teachers attended a postsecondary institution outside of Louisiana, and more than half of the teachers (56%) have fewer than 5 years of teaching experience. In short, the teaching population is younger, less local, and Whiter than both the teaching population before the storm and the current student population. This pattern is particularly true in schools managed by the RSD—which is the primary focus on the teachers in this chapter. Concerns have been raised by the Louisiana Department of Education (2009) about this demographic gap.

Some of this gap has been created by the influence of Teach for America (TFA)—which recruits young college graduates from top-tier institutions around the country and places them in high-need classrooms. Recruiting and training is the primary piece of the Teach for America budget, according to their website:

> Seventy-nine percent of our costs are related to recruiting, training, and developing our corps members and alumni. This figure includes critical investments in national infrastructure, brand, and strategy that underpin these efforts. (www.teachforamerica.org)

The organization points out here that their recruiting and training activities are part of "investments" in their "brand."

The institutional relationships between Teach for America and New Orleans are complex and deep. According to Carr (2009), the New Orleans RSD maintains a nonbinding contract with Teach for America to hire a certain number of teachers each year. According to some reports, this contractual relationship has continued reliably. In 2014, the Louisiana Board of Elementary and Secondary Education (BESE) approved a $1 million contract with Teach for America to hire 520 teachers to place in Louisiana public schools. As mentioned in Chapter 3, Teach for America recently sought $5 million in appropriations from the state to recruit 400 new teachers.

Institutionally, Teach for America is seemingly politically interwoven with public educational governance in the state. From 2011 through the fall of 2016, the head of recruitment for the regional TFA for New Orleans also held a seat on the Louisiana BESE (Williams, 2016). According to Westerville and Kamenetz (2014), "27 [TFA] alumni are charter school principals in the city, and many others are in leadership positions with related nonprofits." At a national level, Trujillo, Scott, and Rivera's (2017) recent research on TFA highlights its push to recruit, shape, and promote the next generation of educational leaders. Edvertising is an essential component of this charge. Teach for America plays a large role in the teaching and leadership network in New Orleans.

NEW TEACHERS, NEW ROLES

This study is a case study of new New Orleans teachers—specifically those with fewer than 2 years of teaching experience. In order to recruit participants, we used a combination of Patton's (1990) "purposeful sampling" and "snowball sampling" (Merriam, 1998). In purposeful sampling, "information-rich" cases are selected for the sample based on whether "one can learn a great deal about issues of central importance to the purpose of the research" (p. 169). Snowball sampling involves asking participants for recommendations for other potential interviewees for the study.

In total, we interviewed 22 new teachers, representing a variety of backgrounds, experiences, organizations, and schools. Table 6.1 shows the teachers, their years of teaching experience, the schools and organizations with which they are affiliated, and their teaching pathway. The vast majority of these teachers were Teach for America recruits. Two teachers were traditionally certified and were not affiliated with TFA, and another participant applied directly to charter schools rather than going through Teach for America. Many of our participants were teaching at KIPP or ReNEW schools. As noted earlier, these two networks represent a large portion of the schools and student populations in New Orleans. Two of the teachers we interviewed were traditionally certified (noted with a "C" in the table), and several of the participants had taken coursework in education as undergraduates or had a degree of some sort in education (usually a minor) but were not certified. This is noted in the table with an "E." Most of the teachers were in their first year of teaching during the interviews. One teacher had quit his teaching role midyear (noted as 0.5 in the table) at the time of the interview. Even among those who are identified as having taught for 2 years, some had taught elsewhere—so most were new to New Orleans.

Table 6.1. Teacher Participants and Pathways

Partici-pant	Number Years Teaching	School	Teaching Pathway: Organization	Traditionally Certified or Education Coursework Program?
1	1	KIPP	Teach for America	
2	1	ReNEW	Teach for America	
3	1	ReNEW	Teach for America	
4	1	KIPP	Teach for America	
5	1	First Line Schools	Teach for America	
6	1	KIPP	Teach for America	
7	1	KIPP	Teach for America	E
8	1	Collegiate	Teach for America	
9	1	KIPP	Teach for America	
10	0.5	ReNEW	Teach for America	
11	1	Traditional Public School	Teach for America	
12	1	Crescent City Schools	Teach for America	E
13	1	Autonomous Charter School	Teach for America	
14	1	KIPP	Teach for America	E
15	2	ReNEW		C
16	2	KIPP	Teach for America	
17	1	KIPP	Relay School of Education	
18	1	ReNEW	Teach for America	E
19	2	New Orleans Prep		C
20	1	KIPP	Teach for America	
21	1	ReNEW	Teach for America	E
22	2	Traditional Public School	Teach for America	

TEACHERS, TFA, AND CHARTERS IN NEW ORLEANS

To begin to unpack the case, we review the teachers' experiences engaging with marketing through multiple organizations in what is roughly chronological order for a new teacher entering New Orleans. We begin by reviewing the teacher recruitment process, and move from there into their TFA training, charter recruiting, and then finally into their experience as teachers.

We contend that recruiting and marketing for Teach for America are essentially the same activity—two sides of the same sword. For this organization, teacher candidates are the consumer base the organization seeks to expand via marketing, in the form of recruiting. As we will see, teachers are also assessing the charter networks and school marketing and recruiting messages in finding their placements. Once within the schools, we find that teachers report shifting roles from educators to participants in delivering some of those same messages. This occurs, in part because of the institutional emphasis on marketing and recruiting which, at this chronological point, targets a different consumer: students and families.

Campus Marketing: Recruiting Teach for America Teachers

The first step on the path to teaching in New Orleans, for most of the teachers in this study, began with the Teach for America recruiting process. All but three of our participants were part of the Teach for America corps. The TFA recruiting process is usually the first moment in which teaching candidates come into contact with and evaluate the organization through its marketing and branding materials. All but two TFA members interviewed for this study were recruited on their college campuses.

Teach for America's recruiting and marketing was nearly universally described as "intense," with one teacher calling it a "whirlwind." According to the interviewees, advertising for TFA begins on and across select college campuses, using resources such as career services, on-campus recruiters, and even early TFA recruits on campus, to access students who are potential candidates. One teacher described this process:

> I think they do a really good job of recruiting on campus because
> they kind of make it a part-time job for people who have gotten early
> accepted. They work at their colleges as recruiters and just plaster the
> whole place. I remember [my college] was covered in TFA posters,
> and I think it was just one or two people doing it. . . . I don't know
> how they are paid exactly, if it's by the number of people, but they
> personally contact people, and say things like, "I think you'd be great
> for TFA. Would you like to talk about it?"

As noted in this quote, TFA has a substantial and visible presence on the campus of many top-tier institutions around the country. Like others in this study, this interviewee indicated that during recruiting periods, her campus was "plastered" with advertisements and marketing materials for the TFA organization. Participants noted the presence of tables set up with TFA representatives baring posters, pamphlets, and sign-up sheets. Two participants from different postsecondary institutions relayed stories of TFA representatives coming to speak in classes and collecting names of students by passing out sign-up sheets. In this stage, TFA makes their brand visible and occupies a significant share of voice in campus recruiting at many postsecondary institutions.

Often, however, as the teacher notes above, the TFA recruiting process began without any initiation on the part of then students (now teachers) themselves. In the above quote, the teacher posits that recruiters might be paid to register applicants on campuses, which incentivizes them to reach out independent of expressed interest. Stories from teachers who had attended other colleges supported this hypothesis. One teacher reported that a TFA recruiter called her directly, but she did not know how the recruiter had accessed her phone number, as she had never signed up with TFA. Another teacher echoed this recruitment story:

> I started to get recruited by TFA early in the fall. . . . They were just, like, really recruiting me, and they were like, "Well, you know, even if you don't end up taking it, you should at least apply, you know, see the process." . . . The recruiter who was on [my college] campus, she was like, "Oh, meet with me." But when I met with her it was just more about how to apply and what the deadlines were and stuff.

Despite having not responded to initial recruitment with interest, this teacher's TFA recruiter told this student to "at least apply" in order to "see the process." Later she was called in to meet with the campus recruiter for what she thought was an information session about TFA, but it turned out to be an application walk-through.

Seemingly, recruiters and their on-campus presence play a crucial role in advertising the organization to student candidates. They reach out to students independent of the candidate's communicated interest, and are tasked with executing campus-wide marketing including "plastering" campuses with advertising materials. Such marketing is widespread and strategically executed.

Many teacher candidates buttressed these initial points of contact with their own online research. Frequently, social media platforms served as a primary informational marketing tool for both TFA, and later for the CMOs these teachers joined. Similarly, many TFA candidates reported relying on videos on organizational websites and social media to assess TFA as an organization. One teacher reported: "I dug through most of their website when I was applying. . . . I watched a bunch of videos." Another teacher indicated that he had gone through TFA's social media sites to prep for interviews once he progressed into the application stage.

Reinforcement from friends or peer alums on social media helped to convince several applicants. One teacher reported that she knew about TFA from campus presence, but initially began to think of personally applying to TFA when she heard about a "distant friend" on social media having been accepted into the corps: "[My friend] had gotten into Teach for America, and I was like, 'Oh my gosh, I've heard about, you know, Obama posting about Teach for America.'" Here, not only did social media play a role in communicating the social acceptance of TFA among this teacher's peers, but also messaging via social media from the Obama administration resonated with this candidate. In marketing terms, this teacher associated the brand of Teach for America with its acceptance and endorsement by the Obama administration—a key selling point for her.

Segmenting the TFA Marketing Messages

Once these student candidates were engaged with TFA's application process to some degree, the advertising messages they received from organizational representatives suggested TFA was adapting its marketing message to suit its perceived consumer.

TFA seemingly altered its recruiting messaging depending on the degrees of engagement from particular candidates. Although several teachers in this study had completed educational coursework before applying to TFA, many had no experience in the classroom or even a particular interest in education leading up to their candidacy with TFA. Multiple applicants reported that, in marketing the organization, TFA indicated that a lack of educational background was not a problem: "They market themselves as, 'Oh, it doesn't matter what your background is.'" Others suggested that TFA representatives simply refused to take hesitation or a lack of interest as reason to disengage in the recruiting process. For example, one teacher stated that her decision to apply was based on a campus recruiter's persuasiveness, stating, "She [the recruiter] convinced me that TFA was where I wanted to go." This convincing of the consumer of their needs echoes Dawar's (2013) quote from Steve Jobs, as noted in Chapter 1. We will discuss this again later.

Other teachers indicated that they believed that TFA strategically adapted their marketing message to candidates based on the organization's perception of the college campus or individual candidate. One teacher indicated that she believed, based on her discussions with other teachers once she entered regional training, that TFA changed messages based on perceptions of political leaning on campus:

I think they do a really good job of saying it's not like, "Oh, go into a city and help the poor kids." Especially at [my college], a lot of people would not be down for that. Unfortunately, I do feel like that was marketed towards some people [on other college campuses] that do join TFA. Kind of like, "Oh, like, go to Africa for a week and help the homeless." Like, you know, a shelter. That kind of thing. It feels like TFA does a little bit of that marketing but they know who to target for that, which is kind of dirty, but they get a lot of people into the classroom.

This teacher contended that TFA does "a really good job" of changing the marketing message for different colleges. On college campuses where the student population would politically "not be down" with a "missionary" agenda as a reason for signing up with TFA, the organization steers away from that rhetoric. On the politically liberal, New England college campus that this teacher attended, viewing TFA as missionary work would likely be perceived as problematically linked to racial inequities and injustice. On other campuses, however, this teacher's perception was that the missionary rhetoric was a primary marketing message. She concludes that this marketing adaptation is "targeted" for the population, which she states "is kind of dirty." However, she attributes this type of market segmentation as being based on the organization's need to recruit as many candidates (consumers) as possible—to manufacture demand.

Another teacher echoed this observation, but felt that TFA adapted for individuals—not just at the campus level:

I think a lot of it is they try to do through interpersonal-type things, emerging subversively in conversations, kind of learning what you're packin', and what your ambitions and goals are, then seeing how they can sell you on the organization in a way that lines up with where you are and where you want to go.

This teacher indicates that he felt that TFA representatives would learn a candidate's motivation for applying, and then "sell you on the organization in a way that lines up with where you are and where you want to go." This echoes the adaptation strategy but on an individual candidate level, rather than based on college campuses.

This personalized segmentation of consumers might be viewed as a positive selling strategy. However, significantly, neither of these teachers indicates that TFA is simply highlighting aspects of their organization that fit different candidates' needs in order to gain interest by showing where their values align. Both teacher interviewees quoted above contend that these are the organization's rhetorical maneuverings crafted with the intention of increasing the consumer base. With the advantage of hindsight, the perception of these teachers was that they were sold something.

In a similar vein, another teacher reported that from her perspective her recruiters shaped messaging to address her particular concerns. During her recruiting process, this teacher had expressed hesitancy to TFA about moving to an unknown city. In response, the organization emphasized to her the impermanence of a TFA teaching position, which she found problematic:

> And this is a huge problem I have with TFA, they kept saying, "It's only 2 years. It's only 2 years." And so now that I'm down here and I see the teacher turnover rate, and I know that the reason for the marketing push is because of that. . . . I think it's a disservice to sell a location, sell an occupation, a profession, a community for 2 years and the way that they treat teachers is that they are only going to be there for 2 years so, like, let's get as much as we can out of them.

By saying "it's only 2 years," TFA attempted to entice this teacher by minimizing the commitment of teaching. Ultimately, this teacher equated the intense and adapted "marketing push" with a selling technique, which she viewed as a "disservice," and that she contended contributed to subsequent high teacher turnover.

"And It Was Kind of Like, Surrender or Else": Becoming TFA Corps

Once candidates were given offers of acceptance from TFA, however, the organization seemingly ceased adapting to and segmenting the candidates. This shift toward alignment can be interpreted as the organization (TFA) seeking to indoctrinate members around a standardized brand and messaging. Thus, although candidates were sometimes drawn to TFA based on intentionally varied marketing messages, at the end of the day, in order to maintain standardized national brand identity, the organization ran them through a process of "voice" and "values" alignment—they were expected to adopt the rhetoric of TFA. From this point on, multiple teachers complained about the lack of flexibility from TFA regarding placement and training schedules and/or timelines, and discussed standardized practices as "Institute" training.

For several teachers, the first signs of this shift came immediately after acceptance to TFA. Teachers reported that the time period from receiving letters of acceptance into TFA corps to accepting a placement was extraordinarily brief and the sense of urgency from the organization was extremely intense. Most teacher interviewees indicated that they had only a few days or weeks to decide whether to accept TFA's offer. In one extreme case, a teacher stated that she had only "1 hour to decide" whether to accept.

Teachers reported that any hesitancy in accepting TFA's employment offer was met with intense pressure. For example, one teacher relayed this story of TFA's approach during her decisionmaking:

I was getting all pressured from them and, you know, I didn't want to make a decision based on anyone else's idea of what I should do, especially teaching. . . . Phone calls were coming from the New Orleans TFA office. I can't even tell you. I probably spoke with like six different people, like, I mean, several of them multiple times. It was just this really huge push to get me to accept the offer. And I remember being really overwhelmed with that, and actually, that was like the first time I had this sense of, "Oh, what kind of organization am I joining?" You know? It just felt bigger and more consuming than just taking a job with an organization and becoming a teacher for them.

Here, again, we see the TFA recruiting industry mobilize to build demand. This teaching candidate was so overwhelmed by repeated phone calls that she "turned off her phone for the weekend" in order to make her decision. She reflected on her wariness at the time that the intensity of the TFA recruiting pressure was indicative to her of something "bigger and more consuming than just taking a job."

At TFA's regional 5-week training Institute in Atlanta, multiple teachers reflected on the intensity of the training, which involved memorizing standardized TFA rhetoric, values, and practices. Among other things, a few candidates reflected on adopting TFA classroom behavior management practices, as well as rhetoric such as the TFA "cultural pillars" described by one of the teachers: "There are five of them. They are like, 'We are bridgers. We are learners. We are stronger together. We are here for kids.' And then there's one other. . . . They preach them throughout Institute." These types of training practices are clearly aligned with standardizing TFA's brand around a set of values that can be recited by its members.

For many participants, Institute made clear to them that joining TFA indeed went beyond "just taking a job." Many described it as more of an intensive initiation period, where standardized expectations were set. One teacher summarized his Institute experience:

"You got in. You're one of us," like, "Do it now." Yeah, yeah. And it was kind of like, "Surrender or else." Like, "You're TFA. This is intense."

Other teachers echoed this sentiment. While several interviewees appreciated the socializing that occurred among corps members, even those who felt positive about the social community-building component noted the intensity of the experience. Several teachers likened it to an initiation for joining a fraternity or sorority more than teacher training. In fact, very few teachers reported that they drew much on any of the classroom practices learned during Institute. It was clear from these interviews that Institute was a key component of "becoming the organization," and not necessarily of becoming a more effective educator.

Prestige Branding of TFA and Teaching

Ultimately, TFA engages in a form of prestige branding and marketing to candidates throughout. The organization sustains itself by marketing its product (teaching) to "elite" consumers (young graduates of top-tier colleges), which in turn makes the brand of the company and network of alums appear "elite." This cyclical building of brand "eliteness" runs contrary to the societal perceptions and popular rhetoric of the role of teaching in society, which one TFA teacher in this study pointed out:

> The unfortunate reality is, and we're talking about marketing education here, they [TFA] market education in a way that's really desirable for high-achieving people. You know? They are trying to—I don't want to say "professionalize" the profession—but the unfortunate reality is that when I was a high school student I looked at my high school teachers, and was like, "You didn't try hard in school so now you're a teacher." You know? And I'm just being completely honest. . . . What they are trying to do is they're trying to say, "That's not the case. This is the most important job in the country, and we need people who are graduates of top universities and high-achieving people and place them within the classroom. . . . We need to somehow make it so it's a prestigious activity."

This teacher argues that TFA has intentionally tried to shift the social perception of teaching so that it is viewed as a "prestigious activity." The organization, he contends, has effectively managed to market education, and the role of teaching, as "desirable for high-achieving people." From a marketing perspective, TFA has created an "elite" brand in part by co-opting the long-established brands of "elite" colleges and universities. Becoming a TFA corps member is associated with the prestige of the Ivy Leagues, for example.

However, the irony is that, by this logic, only teaching associated with TFA—that is, as a corps member—is "desirable" because it is linked with TFA's branded network. Further, it is not necessarily prestigious for an ultimate outcome of the organization to produce lifelong educators, but rather to connect those corps members to the larger network of leaders in other more "prestigious" industries. By not producing traditional public school teachers, the TFA brand remains a signifier of "eliteness" to alums and even the general public. At the end of the day, many of the teachers in this study were drawn to TFA partly because of this.

"They Gave Us T-Shirts and Everything":
The Charter Recruiting and Marketing Process

Teach for America's organizational message was just one of many that newly recruited teachers in New Orleans were exposed to. Placement at a school involved marketing and recruiting from the schools and charter networks themselves. Several teachers in this study talked about the factors that drew them to specific schools or networks once they arrived in New Orleans.

One recurring inducement to join a school community was the larger, local CMOs marketing their facilities and resources. For example, a science teacher indicated that he was drawn to the KIPP network in part because he was told by representatives that KIPP had financial support for science curricular equipment:

> One part that appealed to me was that it was a national charter. I like that they have the resources of a big kind of network. At least KIPP could reach out a little bit . . . that was one of their talking points.

Here, the teacher refers to KIPP's "talking points," indicating that on some level this teacher was aware that the CMO was strategically advertising itself as being more able to provide resources for his classroom. He added that their "national" status was indicative to him of more resources as well. He later contrasted these perceptions with hearsay about other, smaller charter networks not having similar financial capacity.

Another teacher echoed the marketing resources theme about the ReNEW network: "I think their messaging is 'Come work for an innovative charter system that has one-to-one Chrome Book ratio,' which it does." Again, this teacher cites this as ReNEW's organizational "messaging," which is to say their marketing message. These examples indicate that these teachers were aware of the marketing messages they were receiving, and that they were organizational strategies intended to entice teachers.

As noted earlier, some teachers recounted reviewing online materials of charters and their networks, including videos produced by the charter schools and feeds from social media accounts. One teacher reported, "I love the ReNEW videos," and spoke of several videos that "went viral" and ultimately affected her interest in landing at a ReNEW school.

Two teachers indicated that they connected with the school itself, not the network. One teacher stated that he felt he connected with one school in part because of the branded t-shirt he was given: "I went and toured their school, and they gave us t-shirts and everything." Another teacher visited the building and connected with a specific historical significance of the building, about which a commemorative statue was highlighted by building leaders on her tour. Despite her ongoing affinity for the building, in retro-spect, she called this reason for selecting the school "naïve."

Finally, one teacher astutely pointed out that she noticed that these marketing efforts centered on recruitment, not long-term commitment to educators:

> I don't remember them [the charter network] advertising a lot of opportunities for advancement, so there was no false advertising there, because there really weren't any opportunities, you know. A lot of it was just recruiting the teachers.

This teacher observed a lack of discussion of long-term benefits at the school level, and that in retrospect this was not "false advertising." As will be discussed in Chapter 7, teachers universally reported that the teacher turnover rate at many of these schools was high and, seemingly, expected to be so by the organizations involved in recruiting. Thus, the marketing mes-sage is indicative of the goals of the organization itself—to recruit in order to generate demand, rather than retain teachers.

These findings indicate that teachers are responding to recruitment in a manner not dissimilar from research findings about parent behavior in school selection, particularly when marketing is involved as a primary source of information. Like parents engaging in markets, sometimes there are moments or characteristics that lead a candidate to a particular school, which are outside of academic goals, strengths, or interests. Some of these connections are shaped by marketing and branding, which can be as simple as connecting with a candidate by giving away a t-shirt.

Becoming the Message: Teachers as Marketers

By the time teachers arrive at their school, they are part of several organiza-tional fields (Arum, 2000): Many are part of the TFA corps, and a charter network, as well as their individual school. Ironically, having spent several months aligning themselves with TFA, they are faced with the reality that they now work within a completely different organization.

A few teachers reflected on trying to balance being part of various orga-nizations. One teacher likened this experience to "code-switching": acting or speaking in the way that each organization expects depending on which was present at any particular moment. This "code-switching" was directly related to each institution's branded messaging. This teacher said that he quickly burned out because of it. Similarly, another teacher indicated that he gave up trying to balance the institutions: "I was completely thrown off by having four or five different organizations that I was technically working for. And all of them taught me different things. Um, so after the first month, like, I just threw it all out the window." For the latter teacher, "throwing it all out the window" apparently allowed him to enjoy his teaching in the classroom more than several other participants.

Because of these conflicting messages, and because of organizational roles, TFA messaging seemed to fade into the background for many teachers soon into the start of the school year. With the notable exception of required, quarterly Saturday meetings for TFA members, and the occasional observation by a TFA regional trainer, teachers reported that the immediacy of their school and charter network dethroned the presence of TFA in their daily lives. Almost all teachers reported that even after the intensity of Institute, they did not feel aligned with TFA as an organization any longer.

Instead, teachers felt more clearly aligned with their schools, and others within their charter network—depending on the organizational structure. Many teachers seemed reluctantly aware that they were expected to be representatives of their larger charter networks. Their reluctance was reportedly due, in part, to internal (and sometimes external) conflicts teacher experienced in response to the observed behavior or values of the networks. One teacher stated:

> So, I mean, we are definitely told, "You're representing KIPP when you're wearing these shirts" at all times. And in some ways, I'm a proud part of the brand, because they've aligned themselves with Black Lives Matter and other things I feel passionate about and other times I'm like, "Oof." You know? That I maybe don't want to be known for this aspect of this.

This teacher was aware that the KIPP brand represents a variety of values, including Black Lives Matter. While she was proud of her role in representing this brand as an employee to some degree, other brand associations were less positive in her view. This is emblematic of the challenge of teachers in a new role as organizational representatives and brand messagers.

Brand Messengers: Branding in the Classroom. Among other pursuits, teachers were engaging in marketing with their students—although often they did not recognize it as such (an issue we will address later). These types of engagement with students subtly acclimated them to the brand of the larger organization, and implied the need for their acceptance of its values during their time in the school community.

Several teachers indicated that they were encouraged to have branded interactions with their students. Among participants, KIPP teachers reported branded interactions with the most frequency and, in many cases, professed belief:

The branding, the vision, of our school has never changed. Our mission says, "Work hard. Be nice," which I love. I think that's so important. Um, also, we make our children say, "I belong, you belong, we belong always." . . . We also have some longer things that we make them say that are, you know, I honestly haven't memorized them all.

This teacher noted that KIPP's brand is imbedded in the classroom experience. This process is not unlike that of the "cultural pillars" learned by the TFA teachers at Institute. KIPP also utilizes a monetary system to reinforce the principles with students. Another KIPP teacher described the link between this system and branded values:

Ultimately they [values] are all around the same idea, which is, um, grit, optimism, teams, and pride. We try to incorporate them into the classroom. . . . You add or take money away from your [student] paycheck based on their behavior. So like, if we add money, the reasons are aligned to the values. So if a student, um, came in enthusiastic about today's lesson, we'll say, "Oh, he had joy. We'll give him a plus four."

These external rewards systems reinforce via the teachers a values system for the students that is interconnected to the branded identity of KIPP.

Scripted branding with students is important as a practice. Not unlike the teacher who noted earlier that the Obama administration's approval of TFA had led her to accept the organization's brand and apply, students (and possibly families, by extension) might perceive their teacher's messaging as an endorsement of the organization as a whole. Yet, ironically, many of the teachers we interviewed did not endorse the values of their larger charter networks; rather, they stayed in their jobs at their schools despite what they referred to as "upper management."

"You're Expected to Go": Teachers as Recruiters. The final way in which multiple teachers become part of the marketing message of their school or network is through the active recruiting of students. Multiple teachers at different schools and networks reported being required to engage in some capacity in new student recruitment. Several teachers noted the need to "have to recruit kids all the time" as part of the larger market-like system in New Orleans. While some were on the streets or going door to door, others were participating in social media campaigns. Sometimes teachers were even expected to reach out to parents "for leads" of possible recruits. All of these activities bolstered school and network marketing practices at no cost to the school. Recall in Chapter 3 that teacher recruiting activities were noted as potentially supporting formally allocated marketing budgets. Teacher recruiting practices also imply teacher endorsement of the brands associated with these schools and networks. More critically, as we will discuss, it problematically shifts the role of teachers in the classroom, and monopolizes time.

Several teachers described the process of recruiting in person—either door to door or at events. For two teachers, at different schools, door-to-door recruiting was expected to either be done during planning, professional development, after school, or on the weekends. One teacher was surprised that this was part of her expected duties:

> [All staff] did have to go out during professional development and essentially go door to door to recruit students. . . . Recruiting into a school was weird to me because I'm used to, like, you go by zoning. You go to a school where you like based off of where you live. I think I was just like, "Is this real?" Kind of comical but you're like, "Is this really happening? Um, yeah."

For this teacher, having the school go out into the neighborhood to recruit seemed "comical," a situation broadly indicative of the role of teachers shifting away from the classroom and education toward being organizational members.

Another teacher discussed the recruiting incentive put in place at her school. Like the teacher described above, this teacher was expected to go door to door during planning periods to recruit students—specifically kindergartners.

> *Teacher:* Right now we are trying to recruit kindergartners. So I go into the neighborhoods where we think most of our families would be and walk around for hours at a time handing out fliers about our school. So, [it's] community outreach. . . . It's after school, and it's definitely during our Wednesday day when we're supposed to be planning, we've been recruiting. . . . If we recruit one kindergartner then we don't have to go do it anymore.
> *Interviewer:* If you recruit one kindergartner, then it stops?
> *Participant:* Exactly, yup.
> *Interviewer:* So I'm guessing you haven't been able to recruit one.
> *Participant:* No.

This teacher's story raises several concerns. First, she indicates that recruitment requires a substantial amount of time ("walk around for hours at a time") and is taking hours away from her planning time. In addition, either the school or the network has structured things so that teachers must engage in recruiting (called "community outreach") until they "recruit one kindergartner," at which point they are relieved of this requirement, and their planning time is returned to them. At the time of this interview (in the month of March), this first-year teacher had unsuccessfully been attempting to recruit a kindergartener. Thus, this new teacher has been without a planning period for an extended portion of her first year of teaching. This is indicative of a larger organizational trend to which we shall return: Recruiting is organizationally more important than high-quality teaching.

Finally, reminiscent of the quote above, and echoing both the community outreach piece in Chapter 2 and the KIPP DC budgets reviewed in Chapter 3, KIPP teachers reported that they are expected to participate in somewhat regular "community outreach" events. Despite the name, as indicated in the previous chapter, these are commonly, among other things, marketing events that create brand awareness and offer an opportunity to recruit families. In New Orleans, teachers play a role in these community outreach events. One teacher reported that at these Saturday events, there is food and bouncy houses, all of which are "provided by the school." When asked whether this teacher went to the events, given that they take place on the weekend, she paused and responded, "You're expected to go." She indicated that it was a school and organizational expectation that teachers are engaged in community outreach. Here again, teachers are part of the marketing message.

While some schools and networks engaged their teachers in marketing via recruiting, other teachers reported that their schools made strategic efforts to build up an online advertising presence. One charter school teacher described a social media marketing initiative that began at her school that year:

> Starting at the beginning of maybe February, our director . . . introduced us to the social media challenge. [It] was intended for teachers to compete in how many people they could get to follow the Instagram and Facebook pages [of the school]. . . . Our job was to essentially recruit. If you got people to follow the Instagram or Facebook page, you were supposed to record it on a sheet by each week. Part of the meeting that really stuck out to me . . . I think it was also printed out on paper, it was like, "We want to be the school with the best social media in the city." And I was like, "That's a really weird goal." Just thinking in relation to the everyday needs in my classroom.

At this school, teachers were incentivized with prizes to recruit social media followers for the school in an attempt to build the consumer, and possibly, donor base. This teacher indicated that the school's goal was to be "the school with the best social media in the city." She voiced in the interview her concern that this is a "weird goal" considering her perception of ongoing classroom needs and supports teachers are tasked with providing. Like the door-to-door recruiting that other teachers experienced, this marketing campaign subtly, but meaningfully, shows the shift in the goals of teachers away from the classroom to marketing.

In general, teachers asked to participate in these marketing and recruiting practices expressed their discomfort with the requirement. One said: "I honestly, I mean, I wish that we didn't have to go out and recruit. I wish that they could find a way to keep and retain students without teachers." Many expressed a degree of disbelief that recruiting was promoted, even mandated, for teachers—particularly during their planning periods or professional development times. Engaging in these marketing activities was fundamentally disjointed from their needs as educators.

The disconnect of teachers as marketers. Finally, one theme running throughout these interviews was that when asked directly about marketing or advertising at their schools, teachers frequently responded that they could not think of any instances of marketing. And yet, many of these same teachers would then talk at length about marketing campaigns in which they were engaged. For example, the teacher who relayed the account above about the "social media challenge" finished telling the story, and then shortly thereafter stated that she "couldn't think of any marketing or branding" at her school. Another teacher reported that teachers do not market to their students, and subsequently told us of having students memorize branded scripts. Yet another teacher said that they do not distribute fliers to the public in the neighborhood, and then nearly immediately afterward related a story about visiting local families and community places with informational fliers.

This disconnect was interesting. The sense was that the teachers viewed marketing and advertising, labeled as such in interview questions, as an activity they would never do in their role as teachers. Perhaps it is because these activities are not only traditionally regarded as private-sector pursuits, but also because they can have negative (sometimes nefarious) connotations. So possibly, some of the dissonance that can be observed in their statements (for example, one teacher asks, "Is this real?") is between their own views of what drew them into the classroom initially and the edvertising activities in which they engage. This "sensemaking" of roles will be discussed in the next section.

"THAT'S A REALLY WEIRD GOAL":
IMPLICATIONS OF TEACHERS AS EDVERTISING ACTORS

As noted earlier, teachers are at the nexus of edvertising: They are both recipients and participants. We find, as we have in other chapters, that edvertising is at the center of a values struggle in education, and teachers are in the eye of the storm. The organizations within which these teachers are imbedded place a heavy emphasis on edvertising, sometimes over other educational or curricular activities or public goals (Labaree, 1997). These "weird goals" are ethical sensemaking struggles that teachers grapple with within multiple institutions. From an economic standpoint, we must reckon, in each of the cases discussed above, with the recurring theme that marketing for the purposes of expanding the consumer base—whether the consumers are teachers or students—is of more value to both TFA and many of the charter schools and networks in New Orleans than the purported product of the company (i.e., teaching and learning). It pushes us to consider that the product of a company like TFA is not, in fact, teaching, but rather the network of alums, or the organization's survival itself.

Most of the teachers in this New Orleans case study were recruited using heavily marketed and branded activities and materials. With TFA, we see an intensive push to market to teacher candidates at the college level, even when there is little indication that these candidates want to teach and will be effective in the classroom. Yet, despite intense recruiting followed by a subsequent standardized training period, TFA falls off the radar for teachers in this study once they are in the classroom. For this reason, it is important to realize that this organization is not equivalent to a teacher union or a professional organization. Their role as an organization for teachers is as a recruiting mechanism for schools, according to these data.

At the time of our interviews, teachers universally reported high turnover rates in New Orleans. For TFA (as well as for the schools it feeds) continuous, intensive recruiting was critical. This ongoing cycle of marketing, recruiting, and turnover of young, inexperienced teachers indicates an economic rationale behind the TFA's organizational decision to invest in marketing, lest the company would not be financially sustainable. In other words, continuous marketing is likely less expensive (or otherwise more valuable to the organization) than investing in and training lifelong educators, and potentially paying increased salaries in proportion.

Later on, however, TFA teachers are presumably able to tap into one critically valuable component of TFA—their network. For the teachers in this study, that potential value has not yet been realized, as they are mostly still in the classroom. We see this value being translated through the marketing messages of the organization in Chapter 7. From the intensive recruiting underscoring to potential candidates that the teaching is for "only

2 years," to training that emphasized building network connections among corps members, to the lack of in-classroom support, TFA pitches its value to its members as being focused on its peer network.

On the other hand, once signed on, teachers are actors within the organizations themselves. To consider the behavior of the organizations in choosing to use teacher time and energy for the practices of marketing and recruiting, we return to our economic theory of the value of goods. We see similar patterns in the experiences of teachers in New Orleans. The most striking example of this in our study is that of the prevalent engagement of teachers recruiting students during professional development, after school, or during planning periods. In these instances, we see a direct conflict between marketing and classroom or pedagogical needs. Teachers are drawn into activities that emphasize organizational gains at the expense of classroom time.

At the receiving end of both of these edvertising interactions with teachers are students. As we have seen in the many examples in this chapter, teachers who work for organizations that place a heavy value on marketing and recruiting may be less supported in developing high-quality classroom practices—at a minimum, they simply have less time to do so. Pedagogical supports are particularly needed for new or first-year teachers—which, ironically, includes many teachers, and even some principals, in New Orleans.

This brings us to the role of teachers making sense of the messaging. Drawing on sensemaking theory (Weick, 1995), we examine how teachers make sense of the marketing messages they are receiving from these organizations and their role in adopting and perpetuating those messages. In sensemaking, "grounded identity construction" provides a lens for how individuals construct self-concept. Through this lens, individuals make sense of their role as part of a collective organization. We see this kind of organizational identity construction throughout these teachers' experiences.

Teachers grapple with interpreting their actions of recruiting students or having them memorize branded scripts as being part of "marketing." Seemingly, as mentioned earlier, using sensemaking as a lens, the disconnect between their perceived role as "teacher" and the various activities involved in marketing the organization creates a cognitive dissonance. And yet, at the same time, many have constructed identities as "teachers" in these particular institutions that require them to adopt the values themselves—hence, the heavy organizational emphasis on creating brand alignment among teacher recruits at the outset of their time in New Orleans. More broadly, when it comes to edvertising, some of these sensemaking negotiations arise from the institutional creation of what is perceived as the perpetuation of a set of "weird goals," which shift expectations for the teachers.

At the end of the day, the long-term ethical impacts for students should not be forgotten. Some of these teachers left at the end of their first year. Others stayed into the second year of their TFA contract. While some of the teachers in this study might remain in public education, statistics suggest that many will likely move away from the classroom and New Orleans. The students, however, will stay in the city's public schools. Unless policy shifts dramatically in New Orleans, these students will every year be given a new corps of teachers; these teachers will likely struggle, in a variety of ways, with their roles, leading to conflicts between the needs of the students and the organizations for which the teachers work.

CHAPTER 7

Net Impressions
Where Rhetoric Meets Reality

Having examined the organization landscape of edvertising from a variety of perspectives to this point, we now turn to the messaging itself. In building a brand or marketing campaign, each of these organizations must decide on a message that projects an image of the organization as a whole. Yet, there exists little research about the messages being communicated via marketing outlets. We contend that this is a major ethical gap in both policy and research.

From a policy perspective, it is clear that the practice of edvertising is far ahead of educational policy that might result in regulation. As public education wades into the waters of private-sector practices of marketing, branding, and advertising, a new relationship with the public has been entrenched—that of the public as "consumer." Many have argued that the policies and reforms of the past 20 years—particularly that of markets—have pushed education toward becoming a private goal rather than a public one (Labaree, 1997), steering for a "functionalist" definition of the purpose of public schools (Baker & Miron, 2015; Lubienski, 2001). Yet we contend that if public educational policies persist in shifting the position of the public to that of consumers of private products, then educational organizations and institutions should be required to follow federal guidelines regarding consumer protection rules and regulations.

The private sector has long-established policy regulations on product messaging. In protecting consumer rights, the Federal Trade Commission (FTC) prohibits deceptive marketing and advertising:

> Section 5 of the FTC Act declares unfair or deceptive acts or practices unlawful. Section 12 specifically prohibits false ads likely to induce the purchase of food, drugs, devices or cosmetics. Section 15 defines a false ad for purposes of Section 12 as one which is "misleading in a material respect." (FTC, 1983)

Misleading material can include oral, visual, or written representations of the existence of some outcome, as well as a failure to disclose information or "perform a promised service" (FTC, 1983).

In judging whether an advertisement is misleading, the FTC evaluates the message "from the perspective of a consumer acting reasonably in the circumstances" (FTC, 1983). This standpoint attempts to judge the product's messaging from the perspective of a "reasonable consumer" of the intended audience. Thus, even if an ad is targeted at children or senior citizens, the FTC would evaluate it for deception from the perspective of a child or senior citizen consumer, respectively.

However, the FTC does not define deception only as requiring the presence of intentionally false statements. Rather, examining an ad from the perspective of a "reasonable consumer," the FTC considers the "net impression conveyed to the public" (FTC, 1983)—that is, the overall impression of outcomes of purchase for the consumer, even if subtly implied. According to the FTC (1983), the review will "scrutinize the visual and aural imagery of advertisements . . . from the principle that the Commission looks to the impression made by the advertisements as a whole." These net impressions of claims made by a company must be backed by "adequate evidence" or else the ad must include disclosures to offset potentially misleading representations.

The net impressions standard—representing the potential gap between image and reality—is taken seriously in major private companies. It is the source of lawsuits and the reason that in-house legal teams review even slight changes to claims on marketing materials. The same does not hold true in education. Yet the stakes for marketing in education are generally much higher than for your average consumer products company, so research in this area is critical.

In order to examine the net impression of a variety of educational organizations, we drew on two sources of data. First, we collected and analyzed a selection of marketing videos from organizations such as KIPP and Teach for America. Second, we revisited the New Orleans teacher data to look at the ways in which they reported that their net impressions of the roles into which teachers were stepping did or did not meet the daily reality of their jobs.

AN ANALYSIS OF EDVERTISING VIDEOS

To get one perspective of the messages echoing in the edvertising arena today, we analyzed videos created by several of the educational organizations highlighted in the book thus far. Having explored the frequency and cost of the production of these types of marketing videos earlier in this text, and having heard from consumers such as teacher candidates that they use these videos as a source of information, we felt the video content offered an opportunity to evaluate the net impressions standard.

Table 7.1. Videos Included in Analysis

Organization	Audience	
	General and Investors/Supporters	*Teacher/Teacher Recruitment*
Democracy Prep	"Work Hard. Go to College. Change the World"	
KIPP	"The Story of KIPP"	"Extraordinary Teachers"
Success Academy	"The Class of Success"	
Teach for America		"The Basics: What Is Teach for America?" and "Teach for America: Helping Students Achieve Their Dream"

For this analysis, we selected several major organizations imbedded primarily in New York City's school market. Many also cross over into other regions, such as the New Orleans educational landscape. Based on the case study conducted in Chapter 2, we used Patton's (1990) "purposeful selection" criteria in choosing which videos to examine. We chose organizations that invested financial and personnel resources in edvertising, based on our analyses in the preceding chapters, and that were cited by their peers and competitors as being brand leaders in the industry in Chapter 2. The organizations in this part of the analysis included KIPP, Success Academy, Teach for America, and Democracy Prep. Among many reasons for selecting these particular organizations, including the reach and power of these institutions in education today, is that we were able to triangulate some of the findings from the videos with data from our other research in these regions. We were thus frequently able to relate our findings back to issues raised at other chapters in this book, thereby expanding on earlier analyses.

We purposefully selected videos that were professionally produced. Given that our earlier analysis points to several main types of edvertising activities, we grouped videos into two broad categories, based on intended consumer audience: (1) more general videos intended for parents, community, and possible investors, and (2) videos targeted more specifically at teachers and teacher candidates. We realize that any potential consumer could access these videos, however, and discuss this in our analysis. Table 7.1 lists the videos examined for this discussion broken into these two categories.

Our categorization of these videos sometimes arose from our analysis, as we will see, and other times was made explicit by the organization. As noted, some of the videos are general in nature, providing an introductory look at the organization and schools. They often center on the mission of the organization. In most cases, these videos are one of the primary videos on the organization's YouTube or Vimeo channel. Other videos expressly focus on teachers—and, presumably, teacher candidates. A few seemingly also target investors and community supporters of the organization, as we will see. However, given our analysis, we found that many of these videos are likely intended for community supporters and investors, as much as (if not more than) for parents.

We approached this analysis as might be done by the Federal Trade Commission in "scrutiniz[ing] the visual and aural imagery of advertisements . . . [for the] impression made by the advertisements as a whole" (FTC, 1983). From a research perspective, for each video, we engaged in discourse analysis. This process involved several steps and components, as videos are complex media. First, we created a list of commonly discussed themes in each video, and counted the frequency of mentions for each. Within these themes, we selected contextual examples we felt best illustrated the language and issues being raised.

Because these were videos, not simply texts, however, we were also able to examine visual imagery throughout. We counted images of graduations and college banners, for example. In addition, we analyzed the videos based on the amount of time budgeted to particular issues. Like a budget, the allocation of time as a resource is indicative of organizational values. Each of these videos is relatively short, similar to having a limited budget. We therefore contend that the issues that each organization values most will get the most screen time in its video. We also considered who the speaker was in our analysis—whose voice was included or represented.

Based on the combination of our time and thematic analyses, we produced a figure for each video that maps out the themes that are raised, the proportion of time devoted to that topic, and qualitative examples of quotes related to that theme.

General Audience Videos

KIPP: "The Story of KIPP." As the brand leader in the world of edvertising, KIPP has many promotional videos, each with a distinct focus. For this analysis, we look at their main overview video: "The Story of KIPP" (KIPP, 2011b). This video creates a powerful net impression of the long-term outcomes success of the organization.

"The Story of KIPP" is the longest of the videos we analyzed, clocking in at approximately 8 minutes. Throughout those 8 minutes, the video moves through what we classify into several broad sections: the introduction to KIPP section, the teacher/leader section, and the outcomes section. In each section, a recurring theme resonates: the emphasis on college—not just matriculation, but graduation. Although large sections of the video are devoted to other topics, such as teachers and leaders (as we will see), within those sections college is mentioned repeatedly as the desired outcome. Our textual analysis of the video found that the terms *college* or *college graduation* or references to a student's college graduation year occurred more than 32 times. For perspective, the next most frequent term in this video—*leaders*—was mentioned just six times. Our count of 32 college mentions does not include the college imagery scattered throughout the video—particularly of college banners. KIPP's website currently reinforces this imagery, with video clips of graduations and students waving college banners imbedded in the home page.

This video moves through multiple phases and topics, as mentioned above. Figure 7.1 presents the thematic progression of "The Story of KIPP." In our analysis of this video, we address its most commonly raised theme: college matriculation and graduation. Not unlike several of the other large CMOs whose videos we reviewed, "The Story of KIPP" video highlighted several KIPP alums graduating from college—not just their enrollment—while other students simply stated, "I'm going to college." Throughout the video are multiple shots of college pennants. A KIPP board member is quoted as saying, "When I got involved with KIPP 3 years ago, it was 'KIPP to college.' For me, the great change is that we went from 'to' to 'through.'" The fact that the speaker here is a board member re-emphasizes the strategic and organizational nature of the college graduation goal.

As a marketing piece, we can infer that the net impression this video would give the average viewer is that students who attend KIPP will attend and graduate from college. In practice, evaluating these claims—college matriculation versus graduation for KIPP students—is challenging, particularly as there are not consistent, publicly available data on KIPP schools. On their website, KIPP reports that 94% of KIPP students graduate from high school, and 81% begin college (www.kipp.org). It is not clear from KIPP's numbers whether this is 81% of the 94% cohort that graduated from high school, or 81% overall. Interestingly, in addition, KIPP reports tracking these rates based on students who attended a KIPP middle school *or* high school, which suggests that some of the students included in these data attended a non-KIPP high school. However, despite some persistent questions about causality, we can infer from these data and other research that many KIPP students are, in fact, "going to college."

In evaluating the college graduation net impression, we reviewed a report released by KIPP in 2011 that assessed the college progression of their first two cohorts of students: 8th-graders who graduated from KIPP Academy Middle School in Houston and KIPP Academy Middle School in the Bronx. This report begins in a somber tone: "It is unrealistic to expect that all students will finish four years of college" (KIPP Foundation, 2011, p.

Figure 7.1. "The Story of KIPP": Video Breakdown

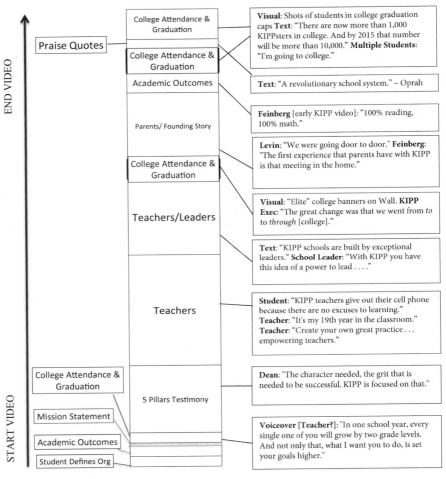

3)—a declaration that runs contrary to the messaging in "The Story of KIPP." The report's findings indicate that "33 percent, of all students who completed the eighth grade at KIPP ten or more years ago have graduated from a four-year college" (KIPP Foundation, 2011, p. 8). Despite that this graduation rate is higher than the national average for low-income students, the findings from this report were, according to a press release published by KIPP, a "sobering wake-up call" for the organization (Bermudez, 2017).

Notwithstanding the findings of this report for the organization, KIPP contends that these data represent only two cohorts at two schools, that it is therefore a small sample size, and does not constitute an overall trend (KIPP Foundation, 2011). Yet the impact of the findings on the organization is clear from its subsequent press release, as well as the follow-up analyses conducted by the organization, including an institutional reconsideration of "summer melt" trends among KIPP alums, and the administration of a survey of KIPP alums in college, which seeks to examines the completion challenges they face while enrolled (www.kipp.org).

Given these findings, the KIPP Foundation (2011) report recommends setting a target of 75% college completion for KIPP students, and also suggests broadening the organization's conceptualization of postsecondary goals:

> At the same time, should students choose paths other than college, whether an associate's degree, a vocational certificate, or a career, we respect their freedom to determine their futures and support them in finding fulfilling work and living productive lives. (p. 8)

While many of these goals are laudable, the rhetoric here substantially deviates from the net impression of the marketing video—that KIPP students will graduate from college. In fact, the overall tone of the KIPP Foundation (2011) report stands in stark contrast to messages in "The Story of KIPP."

Returning to our evaluation of the net impression of the video, the findings from the KIPP Foundation (2011) provide weak support for a broad net impression that KIPP students will graduate from college. Additionally, and perhaps more problematically, it seems plausible that the KIPP Foundation was aware of the findings in the KIPP Foundation (2011) report at the time the video was released—both came out in early 2011.

The timing of the release of the video and report warrants consideration. This indicates that the organization was responding to what they call the "sobering" outcomes and press surrounding the college completion report findings, while publishing a video to market themselves to consumers and donors that gave a net impression that was at least partly inconsistent with their own research. In addition, in the years since the KIPP Foundation (2011) report, "The Story of KIPP" has continued to be one of the main promotional videos for the organization. Given that it has had over 120,000 views on YouTube and Vimeo alone, we assume that the messaging in this video has reached a wide audience.

Success Academy: "The Class of Success." "The Class of Success" (Success Academy, 2016) is the main video on Success Academy's highly branded YouTube channel. As noted in Chapter 3, Success Academy has invested significant money in marketing campaigns over the past few years. In addition, we saw earlier that Success' social media marketing campaign is extremely polished and aligned. Likely due in part to these financial and organizational investments, the promotional videos on Success' website and YouTube channel are of high quality.

Broadly, our analysis of "The Class of Success" is that the video gives an overall net impression that Success' model is an "elite" and dominant reform model in education. More specifically, three main impressions emerge from the video: (1) the "eliteness" of the Success Academy (SA) schools, as evidenced by their facilities and resources, and the visual alliances with highly competitive colleges and universities; (2) related to the "eliteness" claim, the video places heavy emphasis on college graduation, particularly from top-tier universities; and (3) the model as a "proof point" for public education as a whole. See Figure 7.2 for the breakdown of this video. For the purpose of our analysis, we will focus on the main claim of the video: that students from Success Academy will graduate from "elite" colleges.

As indicated by the title ("the class of . . ."), this video focuses on graduation—specifically, college graduation. Simply from the perspective of time usage, as seen in Figure 7.2, like KIPP, this organization seemingly seeks to emphasize not just college attendance, but college graduation. It opens with multiple elementary school students in branded uniforms reciting their college graduation year: "I am the class of 2032," and "I'm 6 years old, and I'm the class of 2031."

Not only does the organization promote college graduation, but more specifically, graduation from very competitive—"elite"—colleges and universities. In this 2-minute video, Harvard is referenced three times and Yale twice. Throughout, banners of Ivy League schools and other top-tier institutions are flashed. Even elementary-age students are seemingly well versed in this rhetoric. For example, near the end of the video, in what is arguably the apex, we see the following sequence:

> *Student 1:* I have the power to make the grades to get into Harvard Law. As a Hispanic woman, I can defeat the odds. I can become anything I want to be. No one can take that away from me.
> *Student 2:* In 10 years, I will be the first one to graduate from college in my family.

[*Flash to banners of Yale, Georgetown, Duke, Michigan, Harvard*]

> *Student 3:* In 10 years, I'll be graduating Harvard University.
> *Student 4:* I want to go to Michigan.
> *Student 2:* Wesleyan.
> *Student 5:* Tulane.
> *Student 6:* Yale.
> *Student 7:* The Ivy League.

[*Flash to wall with two posters: "Class of 2022, Your college application window opens in 17 months," and "Class of 2023: Your college application window opens in 29 months." Wall has printed words "Princeton," "Yale," and "Georgia Institute of Technology." A new screen flashes the words, "Try, Try, Try."*]

Another, closing round of students reciting their college graduation year follows this sequence. This final section constitutes nearly one-third of the video, but the theme echoes throughout. Altogether, approximately half of the video is devoted to college graduation.

Success Academy refers to itself as a "proof point" in public education—that students from low-income backgrounds can achieve academically. In

Figure. 7.2. "The Class of Success": Video Breakdown

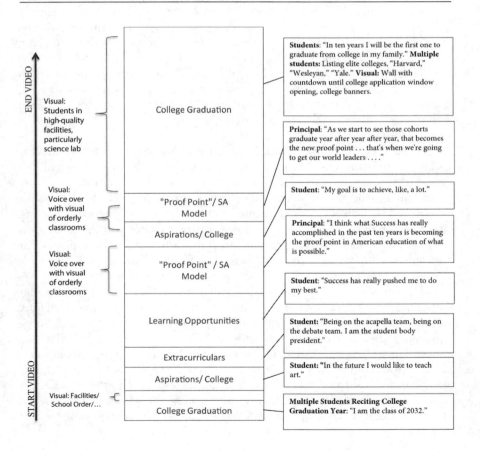

this video, the claim that Success Academy is a "proof point" is wrapped up in the net impressions of college graduation, and even aspirations beyond college. A principal in the video states: "As soon as we start to see those cohorts graduate, year after year after year after year, that becomes the new proof point. They're going to graduate and they're going to go on from there, like, decade 3? That's when we're going to get our world leaders, you know, our amazing inventors and entrepreneurs." Not only does this rhetoric reinforce the college graduation claim ("they're going to graduate"), but it sets a higher target further down the road ("world leaders" and "amazing inventors").

Given this analysis, most "reasonable consumers" watching the "The Class of Success" would receive a net impression that students from Success Academy enroll in, and graduate from, top colleges in the country. We do not want to dispute that Success Academy students may go on to achieve in academia and beyond, and as we will discuss later, we certainly want to endorse holding high expectations for all students. However, from a marketing perspective, this claim does not yet have a foundation in evidence. Simply put, both at the time of the production of this video and at the time of this writing, Success Academy has yet to have a *high school* graduating class, much less a graduating college cohort.

Thus, we assert that the combined imagery and language contribute to this video's precise net impression, which serves a more strictly marketing purpose—that Success Academy is an "elite" institution in its own right. We will discuss this issue later in more detail.

Democracy Prep: "Word Hard. Go to College. Change the World!" Democracy Prep's (2014) video—"Work Hard. Go to College. Change the World!"—is slightly different from many of the others, primarily because it clearly organizes around the organization's mission statement, but also because it is narrated by Dan Rather. See Figure 7.3 for this video's progression. Using discourse analysis to consider the power of the speaker and the impact on an intended audience, the narration by Dan Rather seems to indicate that this video is likely targeted at a consumer other than parents of young children—possibly investors, the public, or even media outlets.

The "work hard" section of the video conveys a net impression that both students and teachers are engaging in intense academics involving long hours. One teacher summarizes their workload: "12 hours a day, going home and grading, investing time in lesson plans, being with our colleagues more than we are with our families or friends." As we will discuss in more detail below, compared with our re-analysis of New Orleans (to come), this net impression seems likely to be an accurate portrayal of the experiences and work loads of teachers in many charter network schools. One can also interpret this teacher's statement as intending to be indicative of teacher "dedication," rather than a difficult work/life balance.

Figure 7.3. "Work Hard. Go to College. Change the World!": Video Breakdown

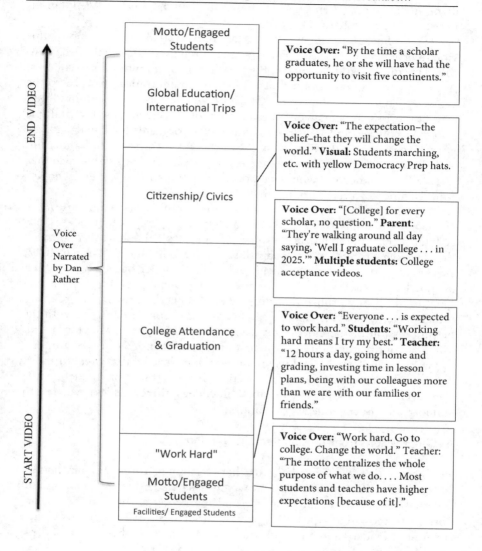

In the "go to college" portion, we hear rhetoric similar to many of the other videos regarding college enrollment and graduation. The voice over (Dan Rather) affirms that college is the expectation "for every scholar, no question." This message is reinforced with multiple clips of students receiving college acceptance letters to competitive colleges and universities, followed by students reciting their college and graduation year. Here again, we get a net impression of Democracy Prep students enrolling in top-tier universities. Further, an interviewed parent in the video indicates that students at Democracy Prep are "walking around all day saying, 'Well, I graduate college . . . in 2025.'"

Unlike Success Academy, it is clear that in 2013, at the time of this video's production, at least one Democracy Prep graduating cohort had enrolled in colleges, and a second cohort was receiving admittances to colleges. According to a grant application filed by the organization in 2016 to the U.S. Department of Education's Office of Innovation: "One-hundred percent of the 148 students who received a diploma were accepted to multiple four-year colleges and universities, and DPPS graduates have matriculated at such schools as Yale, Princeton, Howard, Duke, Dartmouth, Vanderbilt, and the United States Naval Academy" (Democracy Prep Public Schools, 2016). These indicators would support a net impression of "every scholar" from Democracy Prep enrolling in college.

Again, however, college persistence and graduation claims are more challenging to support. In the video, a Democracy Prep teacher states, anecdotally, that the organization's first college-enrolled cohort has "dazzled their college professors." Despite this positive outcome, in March 2017, 4 years after the production of this video, the founder of Democracy Prep acknowledged that college persistence among Democracy Prep alums is a "big, hard, thorny problem" (Toppo, 2017). This rhetoric of the organizational perception of the challenges of completing college contrasts with the net impression of the video. However, Democracy Prep (2016) reports an "88.5% continuation rate for the first group of [Democracy Prep] alumni" —a cohort that had reached its junior year of college by that time. In short, particularly at the time of the production of this promotional video, while there were data to support enrollment in college, there was less evidence to support subsequent college graduation.

Net Impressions from Teacher Recruiting Videos

In Chapter 6, we reviewed the teacher-recruiting process for teachers in New Orleans. One of the ways in which teachers gather information and interact with organizational brands and marketing is through videos, according to those findings. In this part of our analysis, we review two Teach for America videos and one KIPP video that focus on teachers. Both of these organizations are represented in our New Orleans study.

Teach for America: "The Basics: What Is Teach for America?" and "Teach for America: Helping Students Achieve Their Dream." The first Teach for America video, "The Basics: What Is Teach for America?" (Teach for America, 2014) is an introduction to the organization. Figure 7.4 presents its progression.

Using the role of teaching through Teach for America to address "inequity of opportunity" is a recurring theme in this video. One teacher

Figure 7.4. "The Basics: What is Teach for America?": Video Breakdown

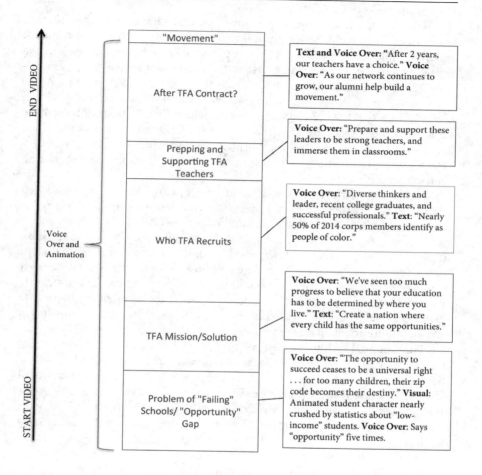

states that Teach for America corps members are "ready take on this idea of inequity," adding that that he is particularly speaking about inequity "of opportunity" that "depends on your zip code." A student reiterates the "opportunity" theme a few seconds later. At the very end, the words *create opportunity* appear on a blank screen.

In using "opportunity" language, Teach for America is positioning itself not only as an educational organization, but as an agent for societal change. The rhetoric of linking opportunity to zip code is commonly found in promotions of school choice policies, like charter schools, which are, as we saw in Chapter 6, closely collaborating with TFA in places like New Orleans. In this video, a priority is placed on the teacher as potential change agent, broadly. Indeed, in the first portion of the video, we hear little mention of classroom practice or education.

Reinforcing this theme of creating societal change, another teacher states that Teach for America "more than anything else is a provocation . . . poking a hole" in the system. It is not totally clear whether the system she is referring to is the educational system or society as a whole, but, as an educational organization, the implication is the former. This "poking a hole" rhetoric is reminiscent of the language of disruption used by jurisdictional challengers (Reckhow, 2013) and organizations like NewSchools Venture Fund (Smith & Peterson, 2006). In fact, overall, these portions of the video give the net impression that the purpose of Teach for America is not necessarily to craft excellent teachers, but to "disrupt" public education and societal inequities.

The video also discusses the teaching role, with one teacher acknowledging he has "leaned on traditional path teachers" to help him during his teaching contract. The video also highlights that being a TFA corps member "starts with a 2-year commitment, and leads to a lifelong dedication to our kids." One teacher describes TFA cohorts as a "lifelong team" of "ultra-driven individuals." With the exception of the teacher who notes that he has sought support of "traditional path teachers," there is, again, little specific discussion of teaching or classrooms. These sections highlight the power and value of the TFA network, and of the "lifelong" membership into a community, which is reminiscent of the findings in Chapter 6.

The second Teach for America video, "Teach for America: Helping Students Achieve Their Dream" (Teach for America, 2015), echoes many of the themes as the previous one—creating "opportunity" and the organizational purpose of creating social change. See Figure 7.5 for this video's progression. The theme of opportunity is drilled at the beginning of this video, with the word *opportunity* mentioned five times in the first few seconds. As in the previous video, this animated short links opportunity to geography: "zip code becomes their destiny."

In discussing whom TFA recruits, the voice over states that they look for "diverse thinkers and leaders, recent college graduates, and successful professionals." They also highlight that "nearly 50%" of TFA corps members "identify as people of color." Here we see, in addition to a push to build a more diverse teaching force, a rhetoric that seeks to recruit not necessarily candidates who are particularly interested in teaching or education, but rather "thinkers and leaders."

Most notably, in these two videos, the experience of the Teach for America corps in the classrooms is barely mentioned. Nor is the particular challenge of teaching in the schools in which TFA members tend to be placed discussed. The only tangible teaching representation is in "The Basics" video when, as mentioned, one teacher reports having relied on support from

Figure 7.5. "Teach for America: Helping Students Achieve Their Dream": Video Breakdown

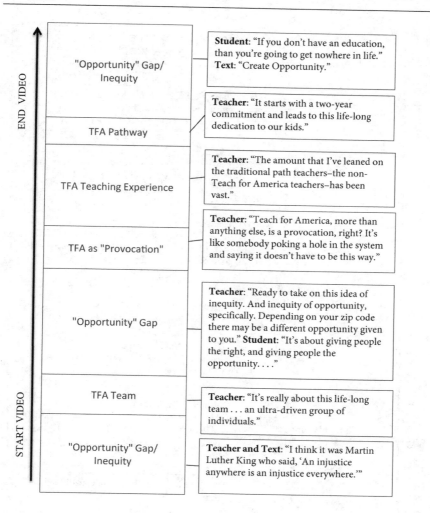

"traditional path" teachers in his school throughout the year. As we will see, this contrasts with the broader experiences of the teachers we interviewed in New Orleans, and with the Democracy Prep video, reviewed previously.

The distinction between the organizational purposes of TFA and Democracy Prep is crucial, however, when interpreting this difference. Unlike Democracy Prep, TFA is not managing schools—their teachers might have a variety of experiences depending on the school in which they are placed. Thus, the net impression of TFA's organizational purpose is not necessarily

Figure 7.6. "Extraordinary Teachers": Video Breakdown

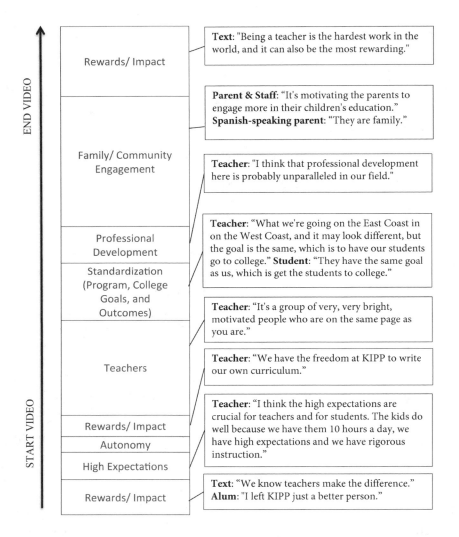

to provide a particular educational experience, but rather to "poke a hole" in the system and build a powerful movement that provides opportunity, broadly, for students.

And yet, as we will discuss shortly, teaching is the job. We argue that this gap between the marketing and the actual experience lived by TFA teachers in the classroom creates some of the challenges reflected in the New Orleans data.

KIPP: "Extraordinary Teachers." KIPP's (2011a) video "Extraordinary Teachers" draws on some of the same footage as "The Story of KIPP," but adds several components and focuses on the role of teachers. Figure 7.6 shows the video's progression.

Some of the rhetoric in this video echoes that of the TFA videos reviewed above. For example, in describing the type of teachers that KIPP employs, one teacher says, "It's a group of very, very bright, motivated people who are on the same page as you are." This section creates a net impression of KIPP's teaching team being a cohort, not unlike the TFA corps. The use of the phrases "very, very bright" and "motivated" subtly signals that many of these teachers have been educated at competitive colleges and universities, and purposely contrasts with popular rhetoric and societal beliefs that traditional public school teachers are not "motivated" or "bright." Another teacher reiterates this theme by stating that she is "excited" that she can "pass her students on" to another teacher at KIPP teacher who "really cares about them." The net impression is that KIPP teachers are an "elite" crew who are higher-quality teachers than your average public school teacher. This is reminiscent of the statement by the New Orleans teacher reviewed in Chapter 6 who said that public school teachers "didn't try hard in school." These organizations seek to market teaching as a prestigious activity.

Also similar to TFA, KIPP positions itself as an organization focused on more than teaching. Another teacher states: "I feel like I'm a really important part of a movement," which places the role of teachers in the context of the goals of the larger organization, like that of the Teach for America videos. The last screen is blank except for the text, "Join the movement," which powerfully and unmistakably underscores this message. The net impression is that teaching is more than for students or teaching itself—it is bringing about societal change, but in the KIPP model.

Unlike Teach for America, however, this video notes the challenges of teaching, although sometimes subtly, and frames them in a positive light. At the beginning of the video, a teacher states, "We have [the students] for 10 hours a day, we have high expectations, and we have rigorous instruction." An astute teacher candidate would infer that the KIPP teachers are also at school for at least 10 hours a day and have a "rigorous" job. Toward the end, text on the screen flashes: "Being a teacher is the hardest work in the world. It can also be the most rewarding." While this statement is open about the challenges of teaching, it frames teaching as rewarding.

Like the more general audience videos, this teacher-oriented video also incorporates the organization's college goal several times. The first vignette includes a KIPP alum (now KIPP teaching intern) stating, "I'm in my last year at Columbia University." Several minutes later, teachers and students reiterate that the "goal" of KIPP is to "get the students to college." These reinforce the college theme discussed earlier.

Finally, KIPP highlights their professional support. One teacher notes that they have "the freedom at KIPP to write [their] own curriculum." This teacher appears to not be a recent college graduate. This statement implies that KIPP teachers are seasoned professionals who have autonomy in the classroom. In addition, another teacher states that KIPP professional development is "probably unparalleled in our field." These statements give the impression of KIPP supporting educators building a teaching craft, and providing unmatched professional support.

"JUST NOT AS ADVERTISED": NEW ORLEANS TEACHERS' PERCEPTIONS OF THE GAP BETWEEN NET IMPRESSIONS AND REALITY

At this point, we return to our data from New Orleans to reflect on the net impression of marketing messages. In drawing on these teacher interviews, we admit that we cannot draw direct comparisons between the videos reviewed in this chapter and teacher data from New Orleans. These teachers were not all employees of the organizations represented in the above videos, nor were they commenting directly on the video content.

Yet, as mentioned in Chapter 6, teachers provide a unique and valuable perspective on the marketing practices of educational organizations at the school level. Perhaps unlike other actors involved in schools, they can see the brand for what it is more clearly than can parents or students. They are both insiders and outsiders. In many ways, their reflections can add to our analysis of what happens from day to day at the schools in which they serve.

The teachers in this data set also have in common having very recently experienced a great deal of educational success in a (presumably) high-quality school setting—having attended some of the most competitive colleges and universities in the country within the previous year or so. This gives them the perspective of the power of education and college success, perhaps more than a parent who has not graduated from high school.

A major finding from the teachers we interviewed in New Orleans is that there is a gap between their net impressions of the organizations they are part of, as processed through marketing and during recruiting and their daily reality. The gap between messaging and the reality of the job for them was significant, often jarringly so, and we argue this contributed to a nearly universal sense of dissatisfaction among participants. In the next section, we review some of these gaps. As mentioned in Chapter 6, these teachers are only a sample, a small subset of a large city's teachers. However, we strongly feel that drawing on their input informs our discussion of net impressions.

On Burnout, Lack of Professional Supports, and Turnover

The most surprising and consistent finding from our interviews was the near-universal report of general dissatisfaction. This dissatisfaction seemingly had a variety of compounding causes. Virtually all teachers mentioned burnout from long teaching hours and a lack of school or network support, combined with occasional mandatory (and unpaid) organizational trainings on Saturdays. One teacher summarized the sentiment: "There's very little help for like, I mean, there's no services." Several teachers noted that the schools were almost entirely staffed by young and under-experienced teachers. A few teachers mentioned that their principals had only one or two more years of experience than they.

Many teachers described the revolving door of young, single teachers burning out due to long hours. One KIPP teacher stated:

> I see that at [our] school, no one is married. No one has kids. It's because they literally dedicate every living second of life to teaching. Which is both great for the kids, but unhealthy in terms of burning out, and not being able to fulfill a very long-term career in this area.

A few participants at other schools echoed this statement, saying they had felt that their teaching roles would conflict with family demands. As a result, several teachers indicated they were planning to quit well before they started a family. One mentioned the lack of a maternity leave policy at her school.

Presumably resultant from this intense workload, numerous participants reported continuous turnover of both administrators and teachers—even midyear—as well as the young age and relative inexperience of both teachers and principals. One of the teachers who was interviewed had already quit midyear. Another participant felt that, because of turnover, the factors that had drawn her to the school initially felt like a misrepresentation.

> I arrived in New Orleans . . . and it honestly was a disaster. They changed the leadership midsummer that I had no idea about. As a result, half of the staff left because they didn't want to work under certain leaderships. . . . So they threw in a whole bunch of new people last second. . . . Everything was new. Just not as advertised.

Despite having toured the school, met the principal, and trained with the network, this teacher arrived and found she was working for a nearly entirely different institution than she had expected. She argues the experience was "not as advertised," highlighting the gap between her net impression of a certain culture with the reality of her experience.

Several of the charter school teachers pointed out that their principals had been teaching only a few years—sometimes only 3—before becoming principal. Because of this lack of experience, several participants who had some background in education or certification recounted instances in which they informed their principal or representatives of a charter network about educational practices, policies, and even laws. This, of course, is the inverse of what we saw in the Teach for America video we just reviewed, which highlights a teacher relying on and drawing support from experienced faculty at his school.

Some participants related their general sense of dissatisfaction back to Teach for America. One teacher indicated she had not realized what she was signing up for when she joined Teach for America: "So [I was] a bit naïve, I think, in following through . . . or maybe I just didn't know much about Teach for America." Another teacher stated that the turnover in New Orleans charter schools was related to Teach for America's continuous re-cruiting: "They rely on a lot of TFA people coming through and so, you know, it makes you dispensable." This teacher states that his impression was that organizations viewed teachers as replaceable because of the power and reach of TFA recruiting practices.

Although this study's sample size is small, the dissatisfaction within the Teach for America Delta Region was reportedly more widespread. Multiple participants noted that at a recent Teach for America Saturday corps region-al meeting, the negative responses to a regional teacher satisfaction survey were reviewed. As one teacher described:

> There was this long survey I guess probably in January, like, "How are you feeling? How are you feeling about being at TFA? How are you feeling about being TFA in New Orleans?" All of these questions. And the response that they got was overwhelmingly negative. . . . The [organization's] response [to the survey results] from TFA was more about sustainability. Like, "Don't quit."

This teacher had the impression that the organization's response to this dissatisfaction appeared to be only about the immediacy of staffing con-cerns; little interest was shown in making tangible changes to create teacher support and enhance satisfaction.

On Combatting Social Justice and Fighting Inequity

Despite marketing claims that many of these organizations are seeking to "poke holes" in inequitable systems, several participants in New Or-leans contended that they felt they were, in fact, perpetuating inequity in schools. One teacher stated: "There are things that might have been said or expressed in trainings or readings, you know, axioms that just aren't true when you get down to the nitty gritty of the organizational level." He went on to recount, as an example, how he was severely reprimanded and nearly fired from Teach for America for missing one day of Institute because of a family requirement that involved his ongoing support for his brother with severe special needs. He argued that this was indicative of the lack of organizational support or empathy for nondominant racial and ability groups.

The above-mentioned lack of resources contributed to the ongoing inability to promote social justice, according to some. One teacher highlighted her perception of the gap between the mission of Teach for America and that of the charter networks in New Orleans, vis-à-vis the dearth of support in her daily teaching life:

> How is this really setting up children for the success that you speak about in that you want to serve them? I sign up for Teach for America and, like, you guys are supposedly about fighting the good fight for social justice. However, the school that you're partnering with whose mission statement sounds really good but doesn't provide . . . the resources I think to fall back on. Just like, being fully employed or like fully staffed. I mean really having the manpower to achieve what they are trying to do, or what they envisioned. . . . It's a lot on the mission statement, which I think is why I was drawn to the school because it's about developing academic success but also with the character building piece. . . . The only vision I see is that they want to be a pre-K through 6th grade.

Here, the teacher contends that Teach for America was "supposedly about fighting the good fight for social justice." In addition, she was drawn to her charter network and school because of the mission statement, which is "about developing academic success but also with the character building piece." Yet, in reality, the mission statements and the messaging of both organizations fell flat for this teacher; she felt the school had a lack of resources to fulfill their vision. The teacher ends by raising an interesting point: "The only vision I see is that they want to" expand their program. Here, we see the conflicting values of needing to provide resources at the school level while simultaneously seeking to expand the school. One can raise questions about the targeting of resources toward organizational goals rather than educational supports.

Echoing both of the above statements, the teacher who quit midyear in our study relayed the following explanation of why he left: "I started feeling like I was sort of, um, perpetuating something that I couldn't continue to be a part of. . . . I think you see inequities in race, class, and gender [inaudible] ways you don't see them anywhere else." This teacher clearly attributed his choice to leave the classroom to his concerns about perpetuating societal inequities, in part because of lack of support. He argues that without the support systems, he was doing his students a disservice, and that such schools are "perpetuating" inequitable patterns both in the city and in broader society.

On the College Preparation Goal

Several teachers lauded the institutional focus on sending students to college, and setting that as a goal. One teacher, however, pointed out his concern about their organizational practices and this goal:

> We do a lot of riding student ass all day. . . . We are really marketing ourselves as college prep. But what's going to happen when these kids go to college and they don't have a teacher breathing down their necks 24/7 like they do at our schools, right? We're not actually giving students autonomy, right?

This teacher argued that the heavy emphasis on behavior management at his charter school network in fact runs contrary to the "autonomy" it takes to thrive in a college environment. Yet, the network is "marketing itself as college prep." Here, the teacher's insider perspective raised the concern that the net impression of college goals can potentially be undermined by school practice of strict behavior management, the type of programming in which many charter networks engage.

On Net Impressions and the Practice of Social Media Edvertising

Finally, we described in Chapter 6 one teacher's account of an incentivized social media marketing and student recruiting campaign at her school. She later discussed the representativeness of the net impression conveyed by these images of students via social media:

> Of course we can snap a picture of an activity in the day that goes really well. And maybe it should be captured, but I think I get maybe frustrated, or whatever, people are trying to paint a picture of stuff is always happening, or like, students always feel this way. Not true.

This teacher raises concerns similar to those unveiled through the research we reviewed in Chapter 1. Particularly, she provides an example of Gewirtz et al. (1995) concept of "glossification." She contended that many photos are of activities that have gone "really well"—the highlights reel— but also emphasized the tension between wanting to document in order to provide information or build community versus trying to paint a glossified picture for the purpose of edvertising.

UNPACKING THE MESSAGE AND REALITY

We begin our discussion of these findings by reiterating two points: First, it is not our intention to argue that any person or institution should hold low expectations for students. As educators, we firmly believe in the importance of supporting students in achieving in all areas of their lives. Yet there's a fine line between holding high expectations and using these scripted aspirations primarily as an advertising strategy to attract consumers. Even larger educational organizations, like KIPP, know that "a brand is a promise." Organizationally speaking, we must assume that the videos have been constructed to convey a set of values.

Second, we reiterate we cannot directly link the data from teachers in New Orleans to the data derived from the video analysis. The teachers were not reviewing the videos themselves, and not all of the teachers worked for the organizations represented in the videos. Yet we feel that the teacher reflections offer some important insights on major themes that emerge, particularly in their role as organizational insiders.

One message that comes through repeatedly in the videos is the desire to build "eliteness." At a basic supply-and-demand level, the more impactful the marketing campaign, the greater the number of applicants, creating the patina of competitiveness and "eliteness" of the institution itself. In several videos in this study, we found organizations striving to project an elite image of the consumer base itself, and aligning with prestigious brands, such as Harvard. This was true for both the general audience videos as well as the teacher-oriented ones. These messages contribute to a cyclical perception of prestige. Research from business schools reviewed in Chapter 1 shows that if one knows that the consumers of a product are elite, the product itself seems exclusive, which in turn attracts more elite consumers. We contend that this demand pattern holds true for education as well.

From the general audience videos, one consistently sees enrollment in or graduation from college being set as a net impression. For some organizations, "promises" of college are seemingly reinforced even at the elementary school level. Our video analysis has raised critical questions about these claims, and highlights the need for distinction between supporting student achievements and using aspirations as publicity fodder. We have suggested that several of these organizational videos have been constructed with the latter motivation.

Particularly in instances in which seemingly little adequate evidence exists to support the recurring net impressions of college and college graduation—often from top-tier colleges and universities—such messaging must be viewed, at least in part, as a strategic marketing move to align the organization's brand with the brands of elite postsecondary institutions. We can see this in the Success Academy videos, where we observe what is essentially co-branding of the organization with Ivy League institutions. For example, the repeated references to Harvard in "The Class of Success" not only create the net impression that Harvard's brand is aligned with Success' brand, but also suggest that Harvard endorses Success' students. There is an implied relationship, when in fact none exists yet.

This elite net impression serves to support the continued survival of the organization when it is shared among gatekeepers (Scott & DiMartino, 2009) and potential investors. Once backed by prominent investors, political support and funding soon follow, which promotes success for the organization. All of this self-perpetuates, regardless of whether students are in fact receiving a high-quality education.

It is also important to consider that videos such as those discussed are but a starting point in building an organization's branded message. A marketing video that reinforces a strong brand can be perpetuated by consumers in word-of-mouth interactions—often as "truth," as now the messages are often interpreted as "known." We see this occurring with the KIPP organization. KIPP's consistent and wide-reaching brand messaging, built on the successes of its flagship schools, led one teacher in New Orleans not to question her father when he told her that KIPP was the best charter network.

The recurring gap between the net impression of marketing and the experience returns us to the major finding of the study conducted with New Orleans teachers: the failure of the reality to live up to expectation. Again, teachers are arguably the best-suited actors to evaluate what is happening at schools vis-à-vis the organizational mission. As we have seen, they apply to many of these organizations expecting to be participants in fighting for social justice in the classroom, and exercising their autonomy as educators, with the financial and organizational backing of multiple well-funded institutions. Simply because they applied to teach in the first place, these teachers were all, at some level, inherently motivated to be in the classroom. However, the day-to-day reality led some of them to quit midyear, and many others to indicate that they were considering breaking their 2-year contract. We contend that the the immense dissatisfaction reported in these interviews is partly attributable to the gap between the reality of the teaching work and the messages that drew them into these jobs in the first place.

When do aspirations and values cross over into simply being marketing ploys? When and how must organizations use caution in constructing the net impressions within promotional messages? These are some of the ethical tensions arising from the application of marketing and advertising in the public sector, and with which we grapple in this book—particularly in this chapter. The possibility that many of these educational organizations were aware of some of these questionable gaps between image and practice, yet elected to proceed regardless, is troubling. These are actions driven by policy, which emphasize private gains over public good (Labaree, 1997). The decisions of organizations to prioritize recruiting are incentivized by the policy structures of market-based reforms we see proliferating today. Shifting our perception of teachers, students, and parents to "consumers" is not just rhetorical—it fundamentally changes their relationship to schools. When seen in this light, investing in the edvertising messaging is completely understandable. Questions should be raised about if, how, when, and why marketized information should be supplied to consumers. The educational sector must visit these issues as it continues to embrace market-like structures and corresponding practices gleaned from the private sector.

CHAPTER 8

Conclusion

The Future of Edvertising

Broadly, this book has captured the landscape of edvertising practices across key organizations and fields within public education, including its leadership and governance, financial supports, strategic initiatives, the use and impact of new technologies, the roles of various organizational actors, and the net impressions of the organizational messaging. It shows the systemic impact of these practices across and within a variety of educational organizations and for multiple consumers. We document shifting resources and examine how organizations construct campaigns and messages, including the growing use of social media. We also see how organizational actors participate in edvertising. From the creation of a new executive class of marketers within public education to enlisting teachers in street outreach, our book illustrates how the embrace of these practices changes the expectations, experiences, and actual work of educational stakeholders.

Given these findings, persistent questions remain about how to move forward, especially since the practice of edvertising is ahead of both the research and policy.

In order to address some of these questions, this final chapter begins with a discussion of several broad themes that emerge from our findings. We continue with two philosophical discussions: the challenging intersection of private and public sectors, and the conflicting role of branding and marketing in choice. We conclude with recommendations for policy, practice, and research.

BROAD THEMES

While our book represents data and research from a variety of perspectives, several broad themes emerge. Here we will look at three of these, drawing on our organizational focus and frameworks: (1) the variation that currently exists in the edvertising industry as it builds steam, (2) the role of privately managed organizations in leading the edvertising industry, and (3) the ethical quandaries arising from our findings on edvertising.

Variation in Edvertising

One major trend that emerges from this book is the degree of variation in organizational focus on, and investments in, edvertising. At a macro level, the regions represented in these chapters are distinct political and organizational contexts in which schools, teachers, and organizations are embedded. These differences account for some of the divergence in edvertising practices.

Yet at a more micro level, we see variation in edvertising implementation even *within* individual districts or regions. Institutional spending on marketing also fluctuates from year to year in many cases. Even in districts where there is intense market-like competition, some schools and organizations are spending a substantial portion of their financial and human capital on marketing and advertising. Others, either for strategic or unknown reasons, appear not to do so.

As discussed in Chapter 3, a portion of the annual fluctuation can be attributed to the nature of the activities surrounding edvertising. Rather than being an operating cost, such practices can be one-time investments that continue to require maintenance, but do not need nearly as much in annual financing. For example, contracting with an outside agency to have a website built or a professional video made is a special expenditure that might skew budgets in any given year. In addition, the creation of a new school—or a new branch within a charter chain—might incentivize an institution to invest in marketing to "get the word out" about their existence.

In addition, there exists a discrepancy in organizational interpretations of what constitutes marketing, which is likely contributing to variation in reporting of such activities. This occurs, in part, because edvertising takes so many forms. As captured in Chapters 2, 3, and 4, edvertising is a multidimensional phenomenon including branding, marketing, advertising, communications, and community outreach, all in the effort to drive enrollment, recruit the best teachers, and in the case of CMOS, burnish an organization's name.

In discussing the field of edvertising as a whole, we must acknowledge these variations. Despite the fact that our research in Chapter 2 points to a rapidly changing landscape, without broader, longitudinal research or data, it is difficult to comment on how trends have changed over time, for example.

Blazing the Trail: The Role of Privately Led Organizations

Despite the differing research foci and geographical regions represented in these chapters, our first broad trend emerges repeatedly: We find that educational management organizations are leading the way in constructing and executing edvertising. This trend particularly surfaces when reviewing the findings on CMOs. In Chapter 2, we show how CMOs form compliance teams to assess brand fidelity at the school level and also highlight the powerful roles of market leaders, such as KIPP, in influencing the entire edvertising landscape. In Chapter 3, as in other chapters, CMOs and charter schools emerged as the clear financial frontrunners for their investments in branding and marketing practices. Even in the extensive market-like structures of New Orleans, the reputations of larger CMOs held power in the national teacher recruitment stream, as they were often associated with having "resources."

Despite evidence of autonomous charter schools making marketing investments throughout these chapters, CMO networks emerge as the dominant force financing such practices. This is brought into stark relief in the case of Massachusetts, in which we can see average marketing budgets of CMO-network schools side by side with their non-network charter peers. The cases of KIPP DC and Success Academy reinforce this spending pattern. However, the budget findings in Chapter 3 represent only the expenses allocated to marketing and branding that are attributable to the individual schools. It is important to mention here that these networked schools often pay management fees to their CMOs, which in turn can use the payments for their own marketing purposes or to augment the school finances. For those institutions with a larger, parent organization at the helm, findings from Chapter 2 indicate that there are devoted in-house expenses for marketing and branding at the foundation level. At the very least, we see executive-level salaries, multi-team marketing departments, and outsourced private contractors being paid for by major educational managers in New York City.

Within the field of CMO marketing, not all organizations are operating at the same level, however. Our findings point to the emergence of several market leaders in the field. We uncover both local and national brand market leaders and challengers in many of the regions studied for this book. As noted above, KIPP is one of the national market leaders. Their brand has not only national recognition, but they have had a clearly aligned brand and marketing message longer than many other CMOs. Longevity in the world of brand-building is powerful—it builds value and trust for consumers. They also have a sizeable in-house marketing team at the foundation level. Their schools and marketing impact touched all of the regions we examined in this book, and other organizational leaders underscored their leadership in these endeavors.

In addition, at a more local level, we see organizations, such as Success Academy, emerging as strong challengers to both the public educational system and the market leader CMOs. We say "more local" because several of these organizations have used their marketing to wade into political advocacy on a broader scale. The case of Success Academy highlights the impact of local, well-funded CMOs and their potential to surpass many of the national CMOs in both organization of, and financial investment in, edvertising.

Findings from Chapters 2 and 3 reinforce the notion that while the public districts included in these studies are shifting some resources toward edvertising activities, even many autonomous charter schools, in cities like New Orleans, are outstripping public districts in marketing spending. Seemingly, public districts are not devoting the same institutional resources to edvertising. Even in districts with vast market-like systems, such as New York City, the central office appears slow to respond, and even perhaps willfully not engaging. As we saw in Chapter 4, in New York City, marketing was primarily used to convey public service messages, such as advertising the school lunch program, rather than as a means to attract new students. Here we see a tension between traditional marketing practices in public education, whose motives reside in civic awareness, and CMO-embraced edvertising, with its focus on market differentiation and competition.

Other major educational management organizations have followed similar patterns in edvertising. Our research on Teach for America, for example, shows an organization that is streamlined and methodical in executing its marketing and recruiting on a national scale. Although its target consumer is slightly different (teachers), it too needs to draw from a wide geographical range and appeal to funders to sustain itself.

The financial investment of CMOs and other types of educational management companies, such as Teach for America, in edvertising is in part an outcome of their greater access to undesignated capital, stemming from investments by private foundations, for example. According to this argument, edvertising is an outgrowth of the organizational autonomy associated with market-based policies and privatization—which is much desired by their advocates, who often hail from the corporate sector. And yet, in Chapter 5, we raise questions about whether the financial capabilities are driving investments in edvertising. Our findings on digital marketing reinforce that not only are CMOs outstripping their public school counterparts, but the marketing efforts are also generally more organized and glossified than elite private schools in the New York City and Boston metro areas. Given that many of the private schools included in this study have access to ample financial support, this indicates that CMOs are strategically making a different organizational choice.

This investment, we contend, is Darwinian in nature, and philosophically based. We argue that the trend of privately held educational organizations blazing the trail in edvertising results from a divergent, but powerful, philosophical belief underlying the purpose of these organizations, as related to parents, students, teachers, and education as a whole. It is not just CMOs but many of the larger educational management organizations, such as Teach for America, that follow this pattern. These purposes relate to the functionalist goals of public education, as discussed by Lubienski (2001) and Baker and Miron (2015), which are outcome oriented in nature and ultimately seek to privatize public education. We will discuss this topic in more detail below.

As privately led organizations lead the charge toward building an edvertising industry, questions should be raised about unintended consequences stemming from it.

Ethical Quandaries Arising from the Findings

Several persistent questions have surfaced throughout our study. Many revolve around ethical dilemmas arising from the growth of edvertising in public education. In this section, we address the following issues: (1) shifting resources of time and money toward edvertising, (2) shifting roles for teachers, (3) the challenges of assessing marketing net impressions, (4) lack of organizational transparency and/or regulation, (6) targeting low-income communities of color, (7) the paradox of the public-sector consumer and prestige marketing, and (8) valuing consumers more than the product.

Shifting Resources: Time and Money. At multiple points throughout this book we see valuable resources—particularly time and money—being allocated to support the activities of edvertising.

The issue of financing edvertising practices has been raised in multiple ways. At the organizational level, we see evidence of budgets shifting to accommodate and prioritize marketing, including salaries for a variety of high-level marketing personnel or recruiters at colleges and universities, and the various activities related to branding and marketing. Referring back to our economic value of goods framework, at a most basic level this is emblematic of organizations valuing edvertising, and using it to communicate value to consumers.

Financing edvertising raises two main issues. First, those organizations with more capital to apply to edvertising are more able to engage in competitive image management in this manner. This creates inequities in which messages are "heard" more loudly, and thus "bought" more often, which are not necessarily related to product quality. Second, shifting budgets, many of which are already strained from underfunding, requires removing funds from some other source (Jessen, 2011). In theory, decisions must be made to reduce funding in another area. This raises ethical quandaries about the activities that are losing financial supports.

In addition to money, time is a valuable resource. At the organizational level, our study shows multiple instances of educational institutions devoting time to edvertising. We see a new organization field, directors of marketing, created to strategize and manage edvertising efforts. Further, the activities outlined in Chapter 4 and 5, such as bus and subway advertisements, social media outreach and web-based banner advertisements, require time to construct and implement. In the case of New Orleans, we see teachers engaging in recruiting instead of being given their planning time. Among other things, this shift represents an organizational value of engaging consumers over supporting educators and students.

Shifting Roles: Teacher as Brand Endorser and Marketer. As mentioned earlier, teachers in New Orleans not only processed organizational marketing messages, but also subsequently became transmitters of various institutional brands and marketing. For example, within the classroom, teachers reported instructing students to memorize organizational branded scripts. Outside of the classroom, teachers participated in recruiting and community outreach events intended partly to create brand awareness.

Teachers play a powerful role for students and families. They are emotional touch points for the school, and often advocate for students. Nonetheless, in these instances, teachers became representatives of the organization. When teachers are placed as organizational members, they must shift their field from the classroom to the organization (Arum, 2000). This raises problematic concerns about the educational activities of and support for the classroom, as well as potential conflicts that can arise.

In addition, teachers' participation in advertising activities carries with them an implication of endorsement—possibly particularly to young students. Yet in many cases the teachers interviewed did not personally feel aligned with the parent organization or charter network. Other times, they outright objected to the organization as a whole. Nevertheless, teachers seemed compelled to follow guidelines, in part to accomplish what had been communicated to them to be "their job." Reflecting on the work of Weick (1995), these young and relatively inexperienced teachers found themselves enacting roles as brand representatives. Only after the fact, in some cases during our interviews, were they able to make sense of their experiences and begin to question their role within their schools and CMOs.

This finding raises questions on whether a more experienced teacher, with a stronger educational foundation, would agree to these shifts as easily.

Grappling with Net Impressions. In Chapter 7 we raised questions about the net impressions of several marketing videos. At a fundamental level, the marketing industry is about message construction. Understanding the degree to which those messages are based in truth is critical. At perhaps its least intentionally deceptive end, consumers can interpret the quality of a product simply from perceptions of marketing investments. These impressions might have little to do with product value. In a more Machiavellian view, advertising activities can be used to intentionally manipulate consumers, including promising outcomes that are not founded in fact.

The advertising industry is ahead of much of the research and all of the regulation. Whereas large consumer packaged goods (CPG) companies maintain in-house legal teams to review all branding and marketing in minutia, the education sector has yet to institute anything similar. We see this as a central concern.

Lack of Transparency. The fact that the advertising industry is being led by privately held organizations leads us to a persistent problem with understanding and evaluating these practices: lack of transparency (Baker & Miron, 2015; DiMartino, 2014). At a most basic level, these privately held companies, unlike traditional public school districts, are not required to comply with open record or meeting laws. This means that everything from budgets to contracts with vendors are managed out of the public eye; not documented for public review. Additionally, many of the documents that are available, such as IRS 990s, are self-reporting, thus eliminating a level of public scrutiny. While these findings are significant for many reasons, with respect to edvertising it makes it nearly impossible to trace investments and practices. This makes holding organizations accountable for their activities difficult. Given the many questions and issues raised in this study, transparency is a critical problem.

Market Segmentation: Targeting Low-Income Communities of Color. As discussed in Chapter 1, research on marketing shows that private companies target marketing campaigns or strategies at particular segments of the population. Given that the majority of charter school students are Black and Latino, marketing campaigns disproportionately target this population of educational consumers (NCES, 2014). Some of these marketing practices are overt, and others much more subtle. In New York City, enrollment in charter schools is most robust in five community school districts, all of which serve low-income communities of color. Advertising executives reported that their CMO clients specifically target these neighborhoods, most notably Harlem, Central Brooklyn, and the South Bronx. Prior to the charter school application deadline, families in these communities receive ads and applications in the mail, and are exposed to an array of ads on buses and street furniture. Given the high level of segregation in New York City's public schools, it is important to reflect on the way these targeted marketing campaigns maintain racial segregation and even exacerbate it.

These overt practices are augmented by more subtle approaches to community outreach. We have emphasized the importance of the community in driving school enrollment. Research shows that word of mouth is one of the most effective ways of shaping consumer preferences; indeed, people often make decisions on the advice of a trusted friend (Bell, 2009; Kimelberg & Billingham, 2013; Oplatka, 2007). But what if that trusted community member is on the payroll of a CMO? What if the grassroots community building in the form of community fairs, movie nights, and ice cream socials is actually part of a coordinated advertising campaign in the guise of community outreach? Returning to our sensemaking framework, how do consumers make sense of these manufactured events created to build their trust in a particular school brand? Further, how do we as a society make sense of such efforts, which primarily target low-income communities of color rather than middle- or upper-middle-class White communities—which in New York City, at least, are just a few blocks away? Edvertising, as currently used, is one of many outgrowths of market-based education reforms, such as vouchers and high-stakes testing, that have the potential to exacerbate segregation (Scott & Quinn, 2014). Paradoxically, if used in a more universal fashion, edvertising holds the potential to be a tool for a more inclusive and less segregated school system. However, to achieve this end, all actors—CMOs and districts—would have to be mutually invested in the pursuit of a more universally equitable education system rather than intent on pursuing their individual agendas grounded in expanding their specific school enrollments.

The Paradox of the Public-Sector Consumer and Prestige Marketing. The term *consumer* in public education is nuanced and warrants unpacking. Public education does not, in a traditional sense, have dollar amounts attached—except, importantly, the tax dollars that follow a student to a particular choice school. Nevertheless, consumers cannot "purchase" in the same way as in the private sector. Moreover, the dollars attached to any student come from a public pool of taxes, not individual contributions alone. Thus, we argue that, in some cases, being a consumer in the public educational realm means choosing to participate in or become part of an organization in a manner that either directly or indirectly sustains the organization—by enrolling in a school, becoming employed by the organization, or donating to it. As noted earlier, sometimes an organization's initial success in recruiting itself becomes a selling point, which garners additional political or financial support.

Yet it warrants mentioning that at least the student consumer base in public education is limited. There are a finite number of students, all of whom must attend school. This is distinctly different from the consumer base for, say, mouthwash. Thus, schools and CMOs are not necessarily competing for more students, but rather for a defined pool of students—sometimes "better" students. Research has shown that markets and accountability create a combustible policy mix that incentivizes schools to try to outperform one another, using choice as an applicant sorting mechanism (DiMartino & Jessen, 2014; Jessen, 2011). Marketing provides a means to target certain populations to create a larger applicant pool from which to draw (Ancess & Allen, 2006; DiMartino & Jessen, 2014; Olson-Beal & Beal, 2016). Concerns have been raised about the inequity in this type of sorting.

In order to begin to segment the student market at the organizational level, we see institutions aligning themselves with other prestigious educational organizational brands, such as Harvard. At a more basic level, repeatedly referring to college might be inspirational, but it could also be intimidating for some students or parents. Among other things, financial means might make the goal of attending any college—let alone some of the most expensive institutions in the country—seem out of reach and deter certain groups of applicants. Even using words like *rigor* or *prep* signals to

consumers the academic achievement needed to succeed at a school (Ancess & Allen, 2006). We found that marketing executives engage in certain
edvertising activities in order to reach target audiences. For example, advertising on certain radio stations will attract one type of consumer. Neighborhood canvasing, which we see teachers undertaking in New Orleans, is
another way of targeting student consumers.

Teach for America engages with a different consumer—graduates of
elite colleges and universities. Teachers among the TFA corps interviewed in
New Orleans perceived that organizational representatives targeted different teacher candidates with distinct marketing messages, depending on its
perception of the candidate's demographic. TFA clearly states that it targets
"high-performing" or "prestigious" colleges in its recruiting practices.

In these cases, the marketing message is targeted with the intended outcome of gaining elite consumers, which serves cyclically to reinforce the
prestige of the organization itself.

Valuing the Act of Consumption More Than the Product. Finally, we argue
that an unsettling thread runs throughout these chapters, related to organizational behavior—placing a higher value on edvertising than education. As
major players in market-like systems, many larger educational organizations
have adopted private-sector rhetoric, in which families and teachers become
"consumers" of an educational "product." Relating back to our economic
value of goods framework, consumers have inherent value in this type of
structure. At its most basic level, without consumers, a company fails.

In order to attract consumers, as we have seen, marketing is critical—
particularly when an organization scales up. Marketing has the power to
construct consumer perceptions of desire (Dawar, 2013), as we saw with the
TFA candidates who were recruited so intensely that they were "convinced"
they wanted to apply and join—even though they had previously not expressed a desire to teach. Marketing can substitute for word of mouth, as we
see with the proliferating edvertising videos, which commonly include parent, student, and teacher "testimony." In a Darwinian system, investment in
edvertising to broaden the consumer base means survival.

Yet, in many cases, the "consumption" that results from marketing is
only the first stage. Enrolling in a school or signing up to teach is just the beginning of "consuming" the good (education). Our findings raise questions
about gaps between the marketing message and the reality of the "product."
Our examination of the net impressions of marketing videos highlighted the
promised long-term outcomes ("through college") of particular organizations contrasted sharply with the stated "thorny" reality of the challenges
faced in trying to support students along this pathway. In addition, through
our New Orleans data, we found teachers reporting a disparity between the
messages that enticed them to "consume" the Teach for America or charter
networks "product" in the first place and the reality of day-to-day teaching.

We are beginning to see an organizational inclination in which institutions are incentivized to value edvertising more than the educational product they are selling. Evidence of marketing budgets and shifting resources supports this theory. In New Orleans, teachers losing planning time in order to recruit students can potentially result in poorer educational experiences for current students. Yet recruiting is given a higher priority. Here, the desire to attract consumers comes into conflict with the quality of the product.

Some will argue that even with the best marketing campaigns in the world, educational organizations would not survive if their products were also not good. In many instances, this is likely true. However, the New Orleans case raises questions about this theory. Teachers simultaneously reported lack of support and burnout along with a continuous stream of new teachers (via Teach for America) coming into New Orleans to fill turnover gaps throughout the school year. While we are confident that many of these teachers are doing good work with their students, we broadly question whether a system structured in this way can provide an adequate or equitable education for students.

As another example, we highlight the case of the teacher who said that TFA effectively markets to make teaching a more "prestigious activity." At the end of the day, the actual product—teaching—is the same whether you begin through TFA or as a certified teacher. Yet TFA's marketing message drew this teacher in despite his stated derision for teachers. Thus, we contend that an organization can construct consumer preferences through marketing. To repeat what Steve Jobs said, "It's not the consumers' job to know what they want" (Dawar, 2013).

PHILOSOPHICAL QUESTIONS

The Private–Public Muddle

The birth of the edvertising industry is resultant of a larger shift in public education. For several decades now, our public educational system has been engaging a slow, yet steady, march toward private management of public education—the trajectory of which has persisted regardless of political leanings of the federal government. It should be argued that the culmination of this movement has resulted in the confirmation of Betsy DeVos—a private wealth-funded philanthropist with no experience in public education—as U.S. secretary of education.

Underpinning this shift are several factors. As Labaree (1997) argued, political debates have pushed the transference of the goals of education from a public to a private good. From this perspective, public education is a commodity to be pursued and "consumed" by individuals. This relates directly to the activities of edvertising, which are critical in communicating with potential consumers.

We have seen a rhetorical transition evolving aimed at altering roles of actors and organizations in public education. Parents and student become "consumers." Superintendents are renamed CEOs. Traditional public schools are referred to as "government run." Yet many private concepts do not transfer perfectly to public education. From an organizational perspective, test scores are not equivalent to profits. Neither teachers nor students are cogs in a machine.

And as mentioned, "consumers" in public education are not traditional consumers. We cannot expand the consumer base of students; we can only divide them among a variety of institutions, which markets require to be unequal. Public education, despite shifting rhetoric and intentions, is not a privately managed industry. It is funded with public dollars from taxpayer pools. This means that "consuming" is a publicly funded endeavor. As a result, the activities of edvertising should be of concern to the general public.

Branding and Marketing as "Discouraging" Rational Choice

Finally, despite many of the questions raised above, some will read this book and maintain that marketing is an inevitable, and even positive, outcome of the introduction of market-like systems in public education. From this perspective, marketing is a sign that organizations are responding to competition, which is a foundation of markets. Choice systems are ostensibly intended to empower parents, and, in theory, marketing is a means of providing information for choices. Yet we argue that, in fact, advertising and the stated purpose of school choice run contrary to one another.

The confidence in markets espoused by many policymakers and theoreticians is buoyed in a belief in rational choice theory (RCT), the central theoretical component of a market-based choice system. RCT contends that people make decisions based on a cost–benefit evaluation of all possible alternatives (Heck, 2004). In an educational setting, RCT suggests that parents are "utility maximizers who make decisions from clear preferences based on calculations of cost, benefits, and probabilities of success of various options" (Bosetti, 2004, p. 388). According to this theory, consumers in an educational choice system will gather information on alternatives, weigh the options according to their interpretation of the best possible outcome, and choose the top schools from among those options. In making a "rational" choice, the dissemination of information is a critical component of any functioning market.

However, in addition to providing information, at a more fundamental level, branding and marketing are intended to elicit an emotional, and perhaps irrational, response from the consumer. We build associations with brands, and perceive investments in marketing as indicators of "quality," for example (Ackerberg, 2001). Whether or not these associations are representative of the truth is not necessarily part of the marketing equation. To what degree, then, do the activities of edvertising in fact undermine rational consumer choice?

In his essay "Brand Meaning," John Sherry (2005) writes, "A brand is a mental shortcut that discourages rational thought" (p. 41). A strong brand triggers quick, instinctual decisionmaking. We buy a particular dish liquid or jam because our parents bought it, for example, or we buy a brand name drug at twice the markup in spite of its generic cousin on the adjacent shelf. Brands and marketing become particularly important in situations in which there is a great deal of choice available to the consumer. Iyengar and Lepper (2000) call these situations "choice overload." They contend that faced with a quantity of options, consumers have a harder time processing the range of alternatives. In these situations, branded identities or marketing messages become a shortcut to choosing as they allow a product to stand out among the range of choices. This is not to say that choosing on brand leads to the most rational choice, however. Thus, brand associations and marketing entice us not to spend the time and effort required for engaging in rational decisionmaking.

We can see how easily this translates to education. In vast systems of school choice, as in New York City or New Orleans, consumers are faced with choice overload (Jessen, 2011). Yet, rather than supporting the process of rational choice, branding intentionally undermines the theoretical foundations on which choice advocates have built market-like systems in education. Instead of processing information, consumers rely on the "experience" conveyed via marketing and branding to attempt to interpret the "experienced good" (Buckley & Schneider, 2007) of education. This is a serious problem if we are to push forward with choice policies and advertising.

RECOMMENDATIONS FOR POLICY, PRACTICE, AND RESEARCH

In this concluding section, we outline specific and targeted recommendations.

Recommendations for Policy

Market-based policies in public education have at this point taken a stronghold in the field. Given the stated agenda of the current administration to continue pushing choice policies, we offer policymakers recommendations that work with the expectation that choice policies in public education are here to stay.

Thus, our main recommendation for policymakers is to take a position of advocating for regulation of the edvertising industry. The history of advertising in the United States is fraught with examples of deception, and consequently an equally robust history of regulation (Petty, 2015). Why should educational marketing be held to a lower standard? Possible regulation could take different forms: It could be federally driven, such as the aforementioned FTC, or it could come from state and local government. It is also within state legislatures' purview to introduce regulatory guidelines regarding their existing charter school laws. For example, as mentioned in Chapter 3, some states already require charter schools, and their accompanying management companies, to disclose their edvertising expenses in yearly financial accountability reports to be delivered to the state. Of course, all terms associated with edvertising—branding, marketing, advertising, and outreach—would need to be clearly defined to ensure accurate and consistent reporting of the data.

Local governments also have tools at their disposal to ensure that organizations advertise responsibly. Local governments often own the land on which outdoor advertising takes place, be it on bus shelters or a ball field. Local government could thus require advertisers to adhere to regulations to protect students. Public health advocates, for example, have pushed local governments to do this for food advertising in and near public schools (Graff, Kunkel, & Mermin, 2012).

Many industries employ self-regulation. In these situations, industries outline their own standards and set up a commissioner or bureau to monitor compliance. Research shows that self-regulation is a useful first step in preventing deceptive practices, but that it must be accompanied by federal and state regulations. Further, the federal and state government must actively enforce said regulation (Graff et al., 2012; Harris & Graff, 2012; Mermin & Graff, 2013; Petty, 2015).

All of these approaches to regulation ought to be applied to public education. Similar to the parental outcry against the Common Core and high-stakes testing, special-interest groups will need to coalesce their efforts in pushing lawmakers to create new legislation and/or enforce applicable current federal, state, and local laws that already exist. For example, New York City Consumer Protection Laws (Consumer Protection Law, 2017) guard against "the use, in any oral or written representation, of exaggeration, innuendo or ambiguity as to a material fact" (p. 4). When viewed through this lens, Success Academy's use of innuendo and, arguably, exaggeration when referencing Ivy League outcomes could be an enforceable offense under New York State's Consumer Protection Laws.

Even as we advocate for this oversight, we acknowledge the complexities of public–private partnerships that need to be considered in any new regulatory effort. Consumer protection laws protect consumers when they actually purchase a good. As noted earlier, in the instance of public education, parents are not directly purchasing a good: No money is exchanged between the parent and the school. In this case of advertising within the public domain, the law is much less clear, which will make it more difficult to regulate these ads. The issue is also complicated because, in the example of Success Academy, we have a nonprofit, private-sector organization that is advertising for a chain of public schools. This intersection of public–private interests has the potential to confound regulators as well as skirt the level of transparency and oversight often associated with the public sector (Baker & Miron, 2015; DiMartino, 2014; Sclar, 2000). This is where public outcry coupled with revised state charter laws can create positive change.

Recommendations for Practice

Our main recommendation for practitioners is to raise awareness. Edvertising is quickly moving from the fringe to center stage, yet few traditional public school educational stakeholders are taking note. The physical changes—street outreach, increased use of direct mail, Facebook pop-ads, to name a few—occur incrementally and seasonally, drawing minimal public outcry. Additionally, the new edvertising positions, such as director of marketing, operate outside of the public eye and traditional education channels. But these changes are here, and akin to the parable of the boiling frog, are slowly altering the nature of public education. We argue that traditional educational stakeholders—district leaders, teachers, schools of education, and teachers unions need more information to fully understand this landscape. Reading this book is an excellent first step in teaching educators about edvertising. But we need to go further.

Schools of education must ensure that their graduates are poised for success in highly marketized educational environments. Teacher education programs as well as undergraduate career services need to work with aspiring teachers on how to negotiate the high-gloss recruitment campaigns described in earlier chapters. Educational leadership programs need to make principals aware of the various edvertising practices taking place in and between schools. Principals thinking about working in highly competitive districts should be offered courses in marketing, especially digital marketing, to allow them to compete with CMO peers. Most important, it is incumbent on these institutions of higher learning to push their students and faculty to, in the words of Weick (1995), engage in sensemaking about edvertising and its associated practices. Now is the time for in-depth philosophical debates about the advent of market-based education reforms and their implications for equity and access within public education.

Recommendations for Research

In Chapter 1 we discussed much of the existing research on branding and marketing in public education. We have contributed to the research base by exploring the cost of personnel associated with, governance structures of, and cumulative impressions garnered by edvertising. We recommend future research in the following areas: parent and student experiences, national variations, and the political nature of edvertising.

We need more research on how parents and students make sense of edvertising. Researchers must examine how parents understand educational markets and the edvertising that results. We need to hear from a diverse array of parents, including those in highly marketized school choice districts and those in adjacent ones. In particular, we need to hear how parents from diverse demographic and economic experiences understand choice and whether their educational decisions are influenced by the activities of edvertising. We need to talk to these parents both before and after their school choice decisions to obtain a better understanding of the factors that influence their decisionmaking as well as their overall satisfaction with their choice once it is an "experienced good." Similarly, students, especially high school students who often have a say in their school choice decisions, must also be interviewed. How do they understand edvertising? How does it influence their decisionmaking and, further, did the hype match their experience? Parent and student voices are a much-needed addition to the research.

Reviews of the literature and our own research show that edvertising practices vary across geographic locations. A national survey of large urban districts would provide instrumental data in understanding national trends: What edvertising practices are being used in various areas, and how much is being spent? This would help researchers determine, for example, whether there is a relationship between the number of schools in a quasi-educational market and increased marketing practices? It would also help capture how practices vary by district, market, and region. A survey directed at school leaders and teachers could encapsulate both the financial resources and time dedicated to edvertising. Such a survey is important to do now as it would provide, in many instances, a baseline on which future practices could be compared.

Finally, we need to further crack the black box of large educational management organizations and edvertising. Our research directed us to links between educational management companies and advocacy organizations. We saw (and experienced at rallies we attended) how Success Academy Charter Schools, Achievement First Public Schools, and Uncommon Schools work together with Families for Excellent Schools, a pro-choice advocacy organization, to further their pro-charter agenda. These organizations band together to orchestrate high-gloss advertising campaigns as well as to foster political action. This nexus of edvertising and political advocacy needs to be studied in greater depth by researchers trying to understand the diverse and powerful actors supporting market-based education reforms.

In sum, our recommendations speak to the need for more robust regulation, discussion, and research on branding and marketing practices in public education. As a direct outcome of market-based educational policies, edvertising pushes public education further into the corporate realm. This shift, which directly affects children, our youngest and most vulnerable citizens, warrants intense examination. It's time for all educational stakeholders—both traditional actors and newer, corporate reformers—to actively debate these changes rather than passively accepting them. These debates, a core democratic process, are essential for sustaining a just and equitable public education system.

Data Collection
for Case Study Budgets

New Orleans

In New Orleans, budget data from both charters and traditional public schools were pulled from the website of the Orleans Parish School Board. OPSB operates both traditional public and charter schools. Of the main governing bodies in New Orleans (described in more detail in Chapters 3 and 6), only the Orleans Parish School Board provides publicly available school budgets (Orleans Parish School Board, 2009, 2010, 2011, 2012, 2013, 2014, 2015). These budgets include a line item for marketing, labeled "advertising."

The "advertising" line item was broken out for the available academic years—2009–2010 through 2015–2016—both for the traditional public schools that fall under the governance of the OPSB, as well as the individual charter schools. For the traditional public schools, "advertising" was included in each year's budget—with the total amount on a summary page, which was then broken down by central office department use (for example, human resources). However, it should be noted that "advertising" budgets for six traditional schools is not reported by individual school, but by the OPSB office as a whole. This is reflected in our analysis.

Unlike the traditional schools, individual charter schools had autonomous budgets from OPSB. These data only began to be documented in the 2011–2012 academic year budgets. Not all OPSB-managed charter schools consistently entered an amount into the "advertising" line item, however. The institutions collected for this analysis represent more than three-quarters (76%) of the charter schools currently managed by OPSB,§ which itself constitutes only about one-third of the schools in the city.

For each school that listed an "advertising" amount in the available years, the line item amount was compiled into the central New Orleans

§ There has been some movement of schools between the OPSB and the Recovery School District since 2013, so the data from available schools are slightly different from the list of currently OPSB-managed schools, by about two schools.

data set along with the "total expenditures" for that institution's corresponding year. These data were matched with student enrollment data, when available.

Washington, DC

In Washington, DC, the analysis focuses on the charter school budgets made publicly available on the DC Public Charter Board website (DC Public Charter School Board, 2016). Because of the format of the budgets, and the inconsistency of certain years, we elected to pull the 2015–2016 budgets from a wide range of charter schools in Washington, DC.

KIPP DC includes 16 individual schools, and the Eagle Academy PCS and the Hope Community Charter Schools network operate two schools each in Washington, DC. The list of charters included in this data set represent 31 of approximately 118 charter schools that are currently operating in Washington, DC, or 26.2% of the charter market in the city. These data are from 2015–2016, and since that year, many schools have opened and closed in the city. Thus, the overall numbers at the time in which these budgets were developed might differ.

The budgets of these charter schools were not uniform in structure or components. In many of these cases, no line item clearly related to marketing or advertising. In other cases, the line item was labeled "student recruitment," and other times annotated as "marketing" or "advertising." Although all of these can be categorized in practice slightly differently, we pulled all related expenses for our analysis.

Of all the charter schools, however, KIPP DC had the most consistent data over several academic years. KIPP DC also represents a significant share of the market in Washington, DC, as it manages 16 charters. For this reason, and also given the political and organizational power of KIPP charter schools nationwide, we pulled budgets for KIPP DC from FY2012 to FY2016 for a closer, longitudinal examination. Of these data, KIPP DC reports three categories of expenditures for these years that we included in marketing/advertising: "student recruitment," "teacher recruitment," and "outreach."

All marketing data were compiled in a central data set and combined with student enrollment numbers when available.

Massachusetts

In Massachusetts, all charter school budgets are publicly available on the Department of Elementary and Secondary Education's website. We downloaded a spreadsheet of 2015 budgets for charter schools in Massachusetts. This data set includes all charter schools authorized in the in the State of Massachusetts during this time period. Each budget has a line item for "recruitment/advertising." Because of the centralized and comprehensive data set, we were able to break down the data for the state by geographic location of each school (Boston, urban non-Boston, suburban, and rural), enrollment, management type, and years of operation. For each school, we also pulled their total expenditures for 2015 (Massachusetts Department of Elementary and Secondary Education, 2015).

Because this data set includes only charter schools, we combed through traditional school and the Massachusetts and Boston departments of education budgets to find marketing expenditures for comparison. We did not find line items for marketing or advertising listed in budgets for either Boston Public Schools or the Massachusetts Department of Elementary and Secondary Education. Because of the complexity of these data sets and websites, we contacted a financial representative by phone at the Massachusetts Department of Elementary and Secondary Education, and inquired about marketing budgetary line items. She confirmed that they do not generally separate this item out, and further elaborated, "It's just not significant enough to make it in [the budget]." As such, we do not have data for schools other than charters.

New York

Finally, in New York, we examined budgets from SUNY-authorized charter schools' Annual Renewal Reports (ARR) from 2012–2013 (SUNY Charter Schools Initiative, 2017). While reports from some other years included financial statements, none were as detailed as the 2012–2013 versions, nor did they include a clearly allocated marketing expenditure.

Even within the 2012–2013 data sets, there was variance in the ways in which recruiting/marketing/advertising was reported. Most frequently, it was reported as a line item labeled "marketing/recruiting." While sometimes this was just entered as a general expense, many times, this was broken down into "student recruiting" and "staff recruiting." We pulled each related expenditure into a centralized data set under three categories: "student recruiting/marketing," "staff recruiting/marketing," and "other recruiting/marketing." In any case in which there was variance in the labels, or a lack of clarity as to whether a line item referred to student or staff recruiting, we entered the amount into the "other" category. To this data set we also added total expenditures for each school and student enrollment, when available.

In all, we compiled budget data for 54 charter schools authorized by SUNY. The largest individual share of the data set was Success Academy, whose marketing and advertising we more closely examined as part of our analysis.

It is worth noting in reviewing these findings that Success Academies has, among its many schools, five schools in the Harlem neighborhood that are grouped organizationally under the category "Success Academies

NYC." These schools had originally been autonomous schools, but in the year leading up to these reports, they were merged. For these five schools, the same aggregate budget was copied into each individual school's report. Since this budget was notably larger than that of all the other schools, we divided the total marketing/recruiting allocations listed in it by five to approximately account for each individual school. It is thus worth noting that our numbers will not precisely reflect the spending per school for the five Harlem Success Academy locations.

Data Analysis

In analyzing the budgets for all of these regions, we examined each regional case separately for numerous reasons. First, we were cognizant that each of these geographical regions has unique approaches to charter development and management, distinct political structures, and diverse demographics and histories within their educational systems. In addition, our data sets represent a wide variety of budget types, sources, academic years, time frames, and definitions. The variances in these data make true, quantitative cross comparisons between the geographic regions impossible. In our conclusion, however, we review broad themes across budgetary allocations and discuss general implications for trends in marketing spending.

References

Ackerberg, D. A. (2001). Empirically distinguishing informative and prestige effects of advertising. *The RAND Journal of Economics, 32*(2), 316–333.

Adnett, N., & Davies, P. (2005). Competition between or within schools? Reassessing school choice. *Education Economics, 13*(1), 109–121.

Ancess, J., & Allen, D. (2006). Implementing small theme high schools in New York City: Great intentions and great tensions. *Harvard Educational Review, 76*, 401–416.

Anderson, G. L. (2009) *Advocacy leadership: Toward a post-reform agenda in education.* New York, NY: Routledge.

Andre-Bechely, L. (2005). *Could it be otherwise? Parents and the inequities of public school choice.* New York, NY, NY: Routledge.

Apple, M., & Pedroni, T. (2005). Conservative alliance building and African American support of vouchers: The end of Brown's promise or a new beginning. *Teachers College Record, 107*(9), 2068–2105.

Arum, R. (2000). Schools and communities: Ecological and institutional dimensions. *Annual Review of Sociology, 26*, 396–418.

Babineau, K., Hand, D., & Rossmeier, V. (2017). *The state of public education in New Orleans, 2016–2017.* New Orleans, LA: Cowen Institute, Tulane University.

Baker, B., & Miron, G. (2015). *The business of charter schooling: Understanding the policies that charter operators use for financial benefit.* Boulder, CO: National Education Policy Center.

Ball, S. J. (2007). *Education PLC: Understanding private sector participation in public sector education.* London, England: Routledge.

Basco, J. (2016, September). Will Austin ISD trustees renew district's marketing plan? *Community Impact Newspaper.* Retrieved from communityimpact.com/austin/education/2016/09/21/will-austin-isd-trustees-renew-districts-marketing-plan

Becker, G. S., & Murphy, K. M. (1993). A simple theory of advertising as a good or bad. Quarterly *Journal of Economics, 108*(1), 942–964.

Bell, C.A (2009). All choices created equal? The role of choice sets in the selection of schools. *Peabody Journal of Education, 84*(2), 191–208.

Bermudez, C. (2017). It's bigger than teaching, it's love: How KIPP is getting students to and through college. KIPP. Retrieved from www.kipp.org/news/bigger-teaching-love-kipp-getting-students-college

Bernard, H. R. (2002). *Research methods in anthropology: Qualitative and quantitative approaches* (3rd ed.). New York, NY: Alta Mira Press.

Bosetti, L. (2004). Determinants of school choice: Understanding how parents choose elementary schools in Alberta. *Journal of Education Policy, 19*(4), 387–405.

Bowe, R., Ball, S., & Gewirtz, S. (1994). "Parental choice," consumption and social theory: The operation of micro-markets in education. *British Journal of Educational Studies, 42*(1), 38–52.

Buckley, J., & Schneider, M. (2007). *Charter schools: Hope or hype?* Princeton, NJ: Princeton University Press.

Bulkley, K., Henig, J., & Levin, H. M. (Eds.) (2010). *Between public and private: Politics, governance, and the new portfolio models for urban school reform.* Cambridge, MA: Harvard Education Press.

Butters, G. (1977). Equilibrium distributions of sales and advertising prices. *Review of Economic Studies, 44*, 465–491.

Carpenter, B. (2014). *Measurement: The key to charter school marketing.* Mount Pleasant, MI: National Charter Schools Institute. Retrieved from nationalcharterschools.org/wp-content/uploads/2014/02/Measurement-The-Key-to-Charter-School-Marketing-140224.pdf

Carr, S. (2009). Recovery School District to lay off dozens of teachers today, *New Orleans Times Picayune.* Retrieved from www.nola.com/education/index.ssf/2009/08/recovery_school_district_to_la.html

Chubb, J., & Moe, T. (1990). *Politics, markets and America's schools.* Washington, DC: Brookings Institution Press.

Consumer Protection Law (2017). Retrieved from www1.nyc.gov/assets/dca/downloads/pdf/about/ConsumerProtectionLawPacket.pdf

Cowen Institute (2016). *The Cowen Institute governance and school guide.* New Orleans, LA: Cowen Institute for Public Education Initiatives. Retrieved from www.speno2014.com/governance-school-guide

Cucchiara, M. (2013). *Marketing schools, marketing cities: Who wins and who loses when schools become urban amenities.* Chicago, IL: University of Chicago Press.

Cueller-Healey, S., & Gomez, M. (2013). *Marketing modules series.* Ithaca, NY: Cornell University Press.

Dawar, N (2013). When Marketing Is Strategy. *Harvard Business Review.* Retrieved from hbr.org/2013/12/when-marketing-is-strategy

DC Public Charter School Board. (2016). School budgets, fiscal audits, and 990s. Retrieved from www.dcpcsb.org/report/school-budgets-fiscal-audits-and-990s

Democracy Prep. (2014). Work hard, go to college, change the world. [Video.] Retrieved from www.youtube.com/watch?v=46f4qSjecHM

Democracy Prep Endurance. (2014). *Annual report.* Retrieved from democ-

racyprep.org/assets/uploads/downloads/Democracy_Prep_Endurance_
Charter_School_2014_Annual_Report_(Redacted).pdf)

Democracy Prep Public Schools. (2016). *Application for grant under the 2016 CSP Replication and Expansion of High-Quality Charter Schools Competition (CMO).* Washington, DC: U.S. Department of Education, Office of Innovation. Retrieved from innovation.ed.gov/files/2016/10/democracy-prepPN.pdf

DiMaggio, P., & Powell, W. (1983). The iron cage revisited: Institutional isomorphism and collective rationality in organizational fields, *American Sociological Review, 48*(2), 147–160.

DiMartino, C. C. (2009). *Public-private partnerships and the small schools movement: A new form of education management.* Unpublished dissertation: New York University.

DiMartino, C. (2014). Navigating public-private partnerships: Introducing the continuum of control. *American Journal of Education, 120*(2), 257–282. doi:10.1086/674375

DiMartino, C., & Jessen, S. (2014). School brand management: The policies, practices and perceptions of branding and marketing in New York City's public schools. *Urban Education.* doi:10.1177/0042085914543112

Drew, C. (2013). Elitism for sale: Promoting the elite school online in the competitive educational marketplace. *Australian Journal of Education, 57*(2), 174–184

Duarte, F., & Hastings, J. (2012). Fettered consumers and sophisticated firms: Evidence from Mexico's privatized social security market. [Working paper.] Harvard/ MIT Public Economics Seminar. Retrieved from http://www.nber.org/papers/w18582

Every Student Succeeds Act (ESSA). (2015). Retrieved from www.ed.gov/essa?src=rn

Federal Trade Commission. (1983, October). FTC policy statement on deception: Letter to chairman on the Committee of Energy and Commerce. Retrieved from www.ftc.gov/system/files/documents/public_statements/410531/831014deceptionstmt.pdf

Foskett, N. (2002). Marketing. In T. Bush & L. Bell (Eds.), *The principles and practice of educational management* (pp. 241–257). London, England: Sage.

Fottrell, A., Katz, W., Reip, A., & Turcotte, S. (2015). The politics of education policy in New Orleans: Student research and policy recommendations. In J. C. Lay (Ed.). *Marketing New Orleans charter schools* (Brief 3, pp. 1–4). New Orleans, LA: Tulane University.

Friedman, M. (1955). The role of government in education. In R. Solo (Ed.), *Economics and the public interest.* New Brunswick, NJ: Rutgers University Press.

Friedman, M. (1962) *Capitalism and freedom.* Chicago, IL: University of Chicago Press.

Galbraith, J. K. (1976). *The affluent society* (3rd ed.). Boston: Houghton-Mifflin.

Gewirtz, S., Ball, S., & Bowe, R. (1995). *Markets, choice, and equity in education*. Philadelphia, PA: Open University Press.

Gewirtz, S. (2002). *The managerial school: Post-welfarism and social justice in education*. New York, NY: Routledge.

Graff, S., Kunkel, D., & Mermin, S. E. (2012). Government can regulate food advertising to children because cognitive research shows that it is inherently misleading. *Health Affairs, 31*(2), 392–398. doi:10.1377/hlthaff.2011.0609 Retrieved from arizona.pure.elsevier.com/en/publications/government-can-regulate-food-advertising-to-children-because-cogn

Greene, J., & Forster, G. (2002). *Rising to the challenge: The effect of school choice on public schools in Milwaukee and San Antonio, Civic Bulletin 27*. New York, NY: Manhattan Institute for Policy Research.

Harp Advertising website (2016). *Branding: Standing apart from the flock*. Retrieved from www.harpinteractive.com/branding

Harris, J. L., & Graff, S. K. (2012). Protecting young people from junk food advertising: Implications of psychological research for First Amendment law. *American Journal of Public Health, 102*(2), 214–222. doi:10.2105/AJPH.2011.300328

Harvey, J. A. (1996). Marketing schools and consumer choice. *The International Journal of Education Management, 10*(4), 26–32.

Heck, R. (2004). *Studying educational and social policy: Theoretical concepts and research methods*. Mahwah, NJ: Lawrence Erlbaum.

Hendrie, C. (2002). KIPP looks to recreate school success stories. *Education Week*. Retrieved from www.edweek.org/ew/articles/2002/10/30/09kipp.h22.html

Hernandez, L. E. (2016). Race and racelessness in CMO marketing: Exploring charter management organizations' racial construction and its implications. *Peabody Journal of Education, 91*, 47–63.

Hill, P., & Hannaway, J. (2006). *The future of public education in New Orleans*. Washington, DC: The Urban Institute. Retrieved from www.urban.org/sites/default/files/publication/51021/900913-The-Future-of-Public-Education-in-New-Orleans.pdf

Holme, J.J. (2002). Buying homes, buying schools: School choice and the social construction of school quality. *Harvard Educational Review, 72*(2), 177–205.

Hoxby, C. (2000). School choice and school productivity (or could school choice be the tide that lifts all boats?). NBER Working Paper No. 8873, Retrieved from http://www.nber.org/papers/w8873.

Hoxby, C. (2001, Winter). Rising tide. *Education Next*, Winter 2001.

Hoxby, C. (2002). How school choice affects the achievement of public school students. In P. Hill (Ed.), *Choice with equity* (pp. 141–176). Palo Alto, CA: Hoover Institution Press.

Internal Revenue Service. (2014a). Form 990: Ascend Learning, Inc. Retrieved from www.guidestar.org/FinDocuments/2015/331/200/2015-331200239-0cbc94cb-9.pdf

Internal Revenue Service (IRS). (2014b). Form 990: Achievement First. Retrieved from www.guidestar.org/FinDocuments/2015/651/203/2015-6512 03744-0cbded60-9.pdf

Internal Revenue Service (IRS). (2014c). Form 990: Democracy Prep Harlem Charter School. Retrieved from www.guidestar.org/FinDocuments/2015/3 00/624/2015-300624890-0cccc310-9.pdf

Internal Revenue Service (IRS). (2014d). Form 990: Explore Schools, Inc. Retrieved from www.guidestar.org/FinDocuments/2015/263/282/2015-26328 2250-0caf4305-9.pdf

Internal Revenue Service (IRS). (2014e). Form 990: Family Life Academy Charter School. Retrieved from www.guidestar.org/FinDocuments/2015/134/17 0/2015-134170389-0c9b90bd-9.pdf

Internal Revenue Service (IRS). (2014f). Form 990: Families for Excellent Schools, Inc. Retrieved from www.guidestar.org/FinDocuments/2015/452/870/ 2015-452870970-0c566ad5-9.pdf

Internal Revenue Service (IRS). (2014g). Form 990: Harlem Village Academies. www.guidestar.org/FinDocuments/2015/223/880/2015-223880680-0cb6e d7b-9.pdf

Internal Revenue Service (IRS). (2014h). Form 990: Carl C. Icahn Charter Schools. Retrieved from www.guidestar.org/FinDocuments/2015/134/166/ 2015-134166657-0cc5e257-9.pdf

Internal Revenue Service (IRS). (2014i). Form 990: KIPP. Retrieved from www. guidestar.org/FinDocuments/2015/133/875/2015-133875888-0ca847b8-9. pdf

Internal Revenue Service (IRS). (2014j). Form 990: New Visions for Public Schools. Retrieved from www.guidestar.org/FinDocuments/2015/133/538/ 2015-133538961-0cb68249-9.pdf

Internal Revenue Service (IRS). (2014k). Form 990: Public Preparatory Network. Retrieved from www.guidestar.org/FinDocuments/2015/264/646/ 2015-264646416-0cc53d0c-9.pdf

Internal Revenue Service (IRS). (2014l). Form 990: ROADS Network. Retrieved from www.guidestar.org/FinDocuments/2015/451/688/2015-4516 88408-0cbf5a53-9.pdf

Internal Revenue Service (IRS). (2014m). Form 990: Success Academy. Retrieved from www.guidestar.org/FinDocuments/2015/205/298/2015-2052 98861-0ccb5e71-9.pdf

Internal Revenue Service (IRS). (2014n). Form 990: Uncommon Schools. Retrieved from www.guidestar.org/FinDocuments/2015/311/488/2015-31148 8698-0cc95bb7-9.pdf

Iyengar, S., & Lepper, M., (2000). When choice is demotivating: Can one desire too much of a good thing? *Journal of Personality and Social Psychology*, 79(6), 995–1006.

Jabbar, H. (2015). "Every kid is money": Market-like competition and school leader strategies in New Orleans. *Educational Evaluation and Policy Analysis*. Retrieved from doi.org/10.3102/0162373715577447

Jabbar, H. (2016a). Selling schools: Marketing and recruitment strategies in New Orleans. *Peabody Journal of Education, 91*, 4–23.

Jabbar, H. (2016b). The visible hand: Markets, politics, and regulation in post-Katrina New Orleans. *Harvard Educational Review, 86*(1), 1–26.

James, C., & Phillips, P. (1995). The practice of educational marketing in schools. *Educational Management Administration & Leadership, 23*, 75–88. doi:10.1177/174114329502300202

Jennings, J. (2010). School choice or schools' choice?: Managing in an era of accountability. *Sociology of Education, 83*(3), 227–247.

Jessen, S. B. (2011). *A year in the labyrinth: Exng the expansion of mandatory public high school choice in New York City.* Unpublished Dissertation: New York University.

Jessen, S. B. (2013). Special education and school choice: The complex effects of small schools, school choice and public high school policy in New York City. *Educational Policy, 27*(3), 427–466.

Jessen, S. B., & DiMartino, C. (2016). Perceptions of prestige: A comparative analysis of school online media marketing [Working paper.]. New York, NY: Teachers College, National Center for the Study of Privatization.

Jones, J. P. (1990). Ad spending: Maintaining market share. *Harvard Business Review.* Retrieved from hbr.org/1990/01/ad-spending-maintaining-market-share

Kamenetz, A. (2015). *The end of neighborhood schools.* Washington, DC: National Public Radio. Retrieved from apps.npr.org/the-end-of-neighborhood-schools

Kimelberg, S. M., & Billingham, C. M. (2013). Attitudes toward diversity and the school choice process: Middle-class parents in a segregated urban school district. *Urban Education, 48*, 198–231. doi:10.1177/0042085912449629

KIPP. (2011a). Extraordinary teachers. [Video.] Retrieved from www.youtube.com/watch?v=3IktN9kzdc4

KIPP. (2011b). The story of KIPP. [Video.] Retrieved from www.youtube.com/watch?v=rVi07IxmVkg

KIPP Foundation. (2011). *The promise of college completion: KIPP's early successes and challenges.* San Francisco, CA: KIPP. Retrieved from www.kipp.org/wp-content/uploads/2016/09/CollegeCompletionReport.pdf

Knight, P., & Hesketh, A. J. (1998). Secondary school prospectuses and educational markets. *Cambridge Journal of Education, 28*(1), 21–36.

Labaree, D. (1997). Public goods, private goods: The American struggle over educational goals. *American Educational Research Journal, 34*(1), 39–81.

Lamberti, C. (2014). *Selling "choice": Marketing charter schools in Chicago.* Chicago, IL: Chicago Teachers Union.

LeCompte, D. M., & Preissle, J. (1993). *Ethnography and qualitative design in educational research* (2nd ed.). New York, NY: Academic Press.

Louisiana Department of Education. (2009). 2009 SPS, DPS, and graduation rates. Retrieved from https://www.louisianabelieves.com/resources/library/performance-scores

Louisiana State Legislature. (2016). NGO funding request from Teach for America. Retrieved from www.legis.la.gov/legis/NGO/NgoDoc.aspx?NgoId=1887&search=ALL

Lubienski, C. (2001). Redefining "public" education: Charter schools, common schools, and the rhetoric of reform. *Teachers College Record, 103*(4), 634–666

Lubienski, C. (2005). Public schools in marketized environments: Shifting incentives and unintended consequences of competition-based educational reforms. *American Journal of Education, 111*, 464–486.

Lubienski, C. (2007). Marketing school: Consumer good and competitive incentives for consumer information. *Education and Urban Society, 40*, 118–141.

Lubienski, C., & Garn, G. (2010). Evidence and ideology on consumer choices in education markets. An alternative analytical framework. *Current Issues in Education, 13*(3).

Lubienski, C., & Lee, J. (2016). Competitive incentives and the education market: How charter schools define themselves in metropolitan Detroit. *Peabody Journal of Education, 91*, 64–80.

Lubienski, C. A., & Weitzel, P. C. (Eds.). (2010). *The charter school experiment: Expectations, evidence and implications.* Cambridge, MA: Harvard University Press.

Marshall, A. (1919). *Industry and trade: A study of industrial technique and business organization.* London, UK: MacMillan.

Marshall, C., & Rossman, G. B. (1999). *Designing qualitative research* (3rd ed.). Thousand Oaks, CA: Sage.

Massachusetts Department of Elementary and Secondary Education website. (2017). Final FY17 charter school tuition and enrollment. Retrieved from www.doe.mass.edu/charter/finance/tuition/fy17/Q4-Final.html

Massachusetts Department of Elementary and Secondary Education. (2015). Massachusetts charter schools: Revenue and expenditure data/ FY2015 charter school end of year financial report summary. Retrieved from www.doe.mass.edu/charter/finance/revexp

Mead, S., Mitchell, A.L.& Rotherham, A. (2015). The state of the charter school movement. Retrieved from: https://bellwethereducation.org/publication/state-charter-school-movement

Menger, C. (1976). *Principles of economics* (J. Dingwall & B. Hoselitz, Trans.). Auburn, AL: Mises Institute.

Mermin, S. E., & Graff, S. K. (2013). The First Amendment and public health, at odds. *American Journal of Law & Medicine, 39*(2–3), 298–307. Retrieved from pubcit.typepad.com/files/mermin-graff_final_4-23-1.pdf

Merriam, S. (1998). *Qualitative research and case study applications in education.* San Francisco, CA: Josey-Bass.

Meyer, H.-D., & Rowan, B. (Eds.). (2006). *The new institutionalism in education.* Albany, NY: State University of New York Press.

Miles, M. B., & Huberman, M. A. (1994). *Qualitative data analysis* (2nd ed.). Thousand Oaks, CA: Sage.

Milgrom, P., & Roberts, J. (1986). Price and advertising signals of product quality. *Journal of Political Economy, 94,* 796–821.

National Center for Educational Statistics (NCES). (2014). Public charter school enrollment. Retrieved from: nces.ed.gov/programs/coe/indicator_cgb.asp

Nelson, P. (1974). The economic value of advertising. In Y. Brozen (Ed.), *Advertising and society* (pp. 43–66). New York, NY: New York University Press.

New York City Department of Education Organizational Chart. (2017, January). Retrieved from schools.nyc.gov/NR/rdonlyres/51A6E9CF-322B-42FE-AEB8-EE3347993994/0/Office_chart_January2017.pdf

New York State Department of Education (2018). Charter school directory. Retrieved from www.p12.nysed.gov/psc/csdirectory/CSLaunchPage.html

Olson Beal, H. K., & Beal, B. D. (2016). Assessing the impact of school-based marketing efforts: A case study of a foreign language immersion program in a school choice environment. *Peabody Journal of Education, 91,* 81–99.

Oplatka, I. (2002). The emergence of educational marketing: Lessons from the experiences of Israeli principals. *Comparative Education Review, 46,* 211–233.

Oplatka, I. (2006). Teachers' perceptions of their role in educational marketing: Insights from the case of Edmonton, Alberta. *Canadian Journal of Educational Administration and Policy, 51*(1), 1–23.

Oplatka, I. (2007). The place of the "open house" in the school-choice process: Insights from Canadian parents, children, and teachers. *Urban Education, 42*(2), 163–184.

Oplatka, I., & Hemsley-Brown, J. (2004). The research on school marketing: Current issues and future directions. *Journal of Educational Administration, 42*(3), 375–400.

Orleans Parish School Board. (2009). Budget office: All charter school expenses (2009). Retrieved from opsb.us/portfolio_office/budget-2

Orleans Parish School Board. (2010). Budget office: All charter school expenses (2010). Retrieved from opsb.us/portfolio_office/budget-2

Orleans Parish School Board. (2011). Budget office: All charter school expenses (2011). Retrieved from opsb.us/portfolio_office/budgets-2

Orleans Parish School Board. (2012). Budget office: All charter school expenses (2012). Retrieved from opsb.us/portfolio_office/budgets-2

Orleans Parish School Board. (2013). Budget office: All charter school expenses (2013). Retrieved from opsb.us/portfolio_office/budgets-2

Orleans Parish School Board. (2014). Budget office: All charter school expenses (2014). Retrieved from opsb.us/portfolio_office/budgets-2

Orleans Parish School Board. (2015). Budget office: All charter school expenses (2015). Retrieved from opsb.us/portfolio_office/budgets-2

Patton, M. (1990). *Qualitative evaluation methods* (2nd ed.). Thousand Oaks, CA: Sage.

PBS. (2002). Interview with Mike Feinberg, co-founder Knowledge Is Power Program (KIPP). Retrieved from www.pbs.org/makingschoolswork/sbs/kipp/feinberg.html

Petty, R. D. (2015). The historic development of modern US advertising regulation. *Journal of Historical Research in Marketing*, 7(4), 524–548.

Posey-Maddox, L. (2014). *When middle-class parents choose urban schools: Class, race, and the challenge of equity in public education.* Chicago, IL: University of Chicago Press.

Ravitch, D. (2010). *The death and life of the great American school system: How testing and choice are undermining education.* New York, NY: Basic Books.

Reckhow, S. (2013). *Follow the money: How foundation dollars change public school politics.* New York, NY: Oxford University Press

Robenstine, C. (2001). Public schooling, the market metaphor, and parental choice. *The Educational Forum,,* 65(3), 234–243.

Rubin, A. (2004). Branded environments: Defining the restructured high school campus. New Visions for Public Schools. Retrieved from www.newvisions. org/node/313/10/1/49

Samuels, C. (2012). District marketing efforts aim to boost enrollment. *Education Week.* Retrieved from www.edweek.org/ew/articles/2012/08/22/01recruit.h32.html

Sclar, E. (2000). *You don't always get what you pay for: The economics of privatization.* Ithaca, NY: Cornell University Press.

Scott, J. (2009). The politics of venture philanthropy in charter school policy and advocacy. *Education Policy*, 23(1), 106–136.

Scott, J., & DiMartino, C. (2009). Public education under new management: A typology of educational privatization applied to New York City's restructuring. *Peabody Journal of Education*, 84(3), 432–452.

Scott, J., & DiMartino, C. (2010). Hybridized, franchise, duplicated and replicated: Charter schools and management organizations. In C. Lubienski (Ed.), *The charter school experiment: Expectations, evidence, and implications.* Cambridge, MA: Harvard Educational Press.

Scott, J., & Quinn, R. (2014). The politics of education in the post-"Brown" era: Race, markets, and the struggle for equitable schooling. *Educational Administration Quarterly*, 50(5), 749–763.

Scott, R. W. (2001). *Institutions and organizations* (2nd ed.). Thousand Oaks, CA: Sage.

Shah, N. (2011). Academic gains vary widely for charter networks. *Education Week.* Retrieved from www.edweek.org/ew/articles/2011/11/04/11charter.h31.html

Sherry, J. (2005). Brand meaning. In A. Tybout & T. Calkins (Eds.), *Kellogg on branding: The marketing faculty of the Kellogg School of Management.* Hoboken, NJ: Wiley & Sons.

Silk, A. (2006). *What is marketing?* Boston, MA: Harvard Business School Press.

Sims, P., & Vaughn, D. (2014). *The state of public education in New Orleans, 2014 report.* New Orleans, LA: Cowen Institute, Tulane University.

Smith, W. (1956). Product differentiation and market segmentation as alternative marketing strategies. *Journal of Marketing*, 21(1), 3–8.

Smith, K., & Peterson, J. L. (2006). What is educational entrepreneurship? In F. Hess (Ed.), *Educational entrepreneurship: Realities, challenges, possibilities*. Cambridge, MA: Harvard Education Press.

Sparling, H. (2016). Selling our schools: With competition on the rise, it's a fight for students. Retrieved from www.cincinnati.com/story/news/education/2016/05/12/selling-our-schools-competition-rise-s-fight-students/83923032/

Stake, R. E. (1995). *The art of case study research*. Thousand Oaks, CA: Sage.

Stewart, M. S., & Good, A. G. (2016). Marketing, information, and parental choice: A comparative case study of third-party, federally funded out-of-school-time services. *Peabody Journal of Education, 91*, 100–120.

Stifler, G. L. (1961). The economics of information. *Journal of Political Economy, 71*, 213–225.

Success Academy. (2016). The class of success. [Video.] Retrieved from www.youtube.com/watch?v=uYnJQOa5TFQ

SUNY Charter Schools Initiative. (2017). School performance reports. Retrieved from www.newyorkcharters.org/progress/school-performance-reports

SUNY website. (2017). About. The charter schools initiative. Retrieved from www.newyorkcharters.org/about

Symes, C. (1998). Education for sale: A semiotic analysis of school prospectuses and other forms of educational marketing. *Australian Journal of Education, 42*(2), 133–152.

Teach for America. (2014). *The basics: What is Teach for America?* [Video.] Retrieved from www.youtube.com/watch?v=QLtKDJWYnr0

Teach for America. (2015). *Teach for America: Helping students achieve their dream.* [Video.] Retrieved from www.youtube.com/watch?v=CzE4N-zLAzF8

Toppo, G. (2017). Charter schools' "thorny" problem: Few students go on to earn college degrees. *USA Today*. Retrieved from www.usatoday.com/story/news/2017/03/14/charter-schools-college-degrees/99125468

Trujillo, T., Scott, J., & Rivera, M. (2017). Follow the yellow brick road: Teach for America and the making of educational leaders. *American Journal of Education, 123*(3), 353–391.

USDOE. (2012). U.S. Department of Education announces grants totaling more than $14.4 million to charter school management organizations. [Press release.]

Venture Philanthropy Partners. (2015). *Expanding educational opportunities for youth: KIPP DC case study.* Retrieved from www.vppartners.org/wp-content/uploads/2016/12/KIPP-DC_Case-Study.pdf

Washington Post (2010). Interactive: Mapping the census. Retrieved from www.washingtonpost.com/wp-srv/special/nation/census/2010

Weick, K. E. (1995). *Sensemaking in organizations* (Vol. 3). Thousand Oaks, CA: Sage.

Westerville, E., & Kamenetz, A. (2014). Teach for America at 25: With maturity, new pressure to change. Washington, DC: National Public Radio. Retrieved from www.npr.org/sections/ed/2014/12/01/366343324/teach-for-america-at-25-with-maturity-new-pressure-to-change

Whitty, G., & Power, S. (2000). Marketization and privatization in mass education systems. *International Journal of Educational Development, 20,* 93–107.

Wilkins, A. (2012). School choice and the commodification of education: A visual approach to school brochures and websites. *Critical Social Policy, 32*(1), 69–86.

Williams, J. (2016, September). Kira Orange Jones, local TFA director, to leave post for larger role in company. *The New Orleans Advocate.* Retrieved from www.theadvocate.com/new_orleans/news/education/article_a414c846-76e8-11e6-ace2-03356f3ff803.html

Wilson, T. S., & Carlsen, R. L. (2016). School marketing as a sorting mechanism: A critical discourse analysis of charter school websites. *Peabody Journal of Education, 91,* 24–46

Yin, R. (2003). *Case study research: Design and methods* (3rd ed.). Thousand Oaks, CA: Sage.

Index

About the Authors

Catherine DiMartino is an associate professor in the Department of Administrative and Instructional Leadership at St. John's University. Prior to joining the St. John's community, she taught middle and high school social studies in New York City, conducted research for the RAND Corporation, and, most recently, was an assistant professor at Hofstra University. Her research focuses on the politics of urban school reform. Currently, she is examining the implications of market-based educational policies on public education. Dr. DiMartino's work has appeared in several journals, including the *American Journal of Education* and *Educational Policy*.

Sarah Butler Jessen is a faculty member at the University of Southern Maine's Muskie School of Public Service. Prior to this, she was a visiting assistant professor of Education at Bowdoin College for several years. Her research focuses on public policies in education, specifically the effects of market-based and privatization policies, as well as the historical and political contexts affecting the public educational system. Her dissertation, which examined the outcomes of mandatory school choice policies in New York City, was a runner-up for the American Education Research Association's Division L Outstanding Dissertation Award. She has published in peer-reviewed journals, including *Educational Policy* and *Urban Education*. She earned her MA in Anthropology of Education from Teachers College at Columbia University, and her PhD in Educational Leadership, with a concentration in policy studies, from New York University.